The
McClellanville Coast
Cookbook

Afloat Again After Hugo, Jeremy Creek, 1989, a photograph by Bernadette Humphrey.

The McClellanville Coast Cookbook

Recipes, Oral Histories, Poetry, Prose, Prints, Photographs,
and Paintings from McClellanville, Awendaw, South Santee,
Germanville, Tibwin, Seewee, Buck Hall, Moss Swamp,
and Honey Hill,
South Carolina

Edited by Susan Williams

Published by the
McClellanville Arts Council
McClellanville, South Carolina

1992

Third printing, November 1995.

Printed in the United States of America.

ISBN 1-882966-00-7

On the cover--McClellanville Mural, St. James-Santee Elementary School. Painted in 1992 by 5th graders under the direction of Artist-in-Residence Russell Everett, this mural measures 14' x 7' and is on permanent display in the Media Center. Photographed by Bernadette Humphrey.

TABLE OF CONTENTS

The Recipes

Butterbeans, a photograph by Bernadette Humphrey.

INTRODUCTION

One of the great pleasures of living in McClellanville is the food. People here earn their livings from food, entertain with food, celebrate with food, and mourn with food. They are always fixing tables full of food for their neighbors in times of birth, death, and sudden need. The same dishes that feed a family at home table are made in larger quantities to feed a church or to feed the crowd at the Fourth of July picnic, so you know you are always eating the cooks' best--the sweet potato pone made from a recipe handed down from generations yet that gets re-invented by everyone who tries it, or the oyster casserole which has passed from one old family to another, through marriage, as likely as not.

Untypically, perhaps, in a rural area where jobs are scarce or underpaid, many people have come here from somewhere else, and they have contributed to the variety of flavors and cooking techniques that have entered the local cuisine. Still, the main ingredients they use are the tried and tested ones. Seafood tops the list. The shrimp, oysters, crabs, and clams caught by men who know their way back to the dock by sight and sound are cleaned and packed by people whose ancestors cultivated rice and cotton in the plantation era.

It was not long ago that people made bulrush baskets to "fan" rice, mortars and pestles to pound it, trunks and gates to control the flow of water on the rice fields. They operated mills to grind their corn and rice. They wove nets and built the boats they fished with. They butchered hogs and cured the meat, using salt they obtained by evaporating sea water. Ask people and they'll tell you their happiest memories recall how all the wonderful local ingredients came together--in good cooking.

In tribute to the old-timers and the newcomers, the McClellanville Arts Council has collected the recipes of both, for the enjoyment of the people who live here and for all those who are not lucky enough to.

Our cookbook was partially funded by the South Carolina Arts Commission and the National Endowment for the Arts through a three-year Rural Arts Initiative grant awarded in 1989, just weeks after Hurricane Hugo ravaged McClellanville. Hugo destroyed our former Arts Center and washed away much of the traditional culture of the area--or so it appeared to us at the time. By the following summer, however, the Arts Council had moved into a new building and had assembled an exhibit called "From Seewee to Santee: The McClellanville Coast," featuring the work of area artists from 1720 to the present. Some of the objects in this show were waterstained or had been recovered from piles of debris. A few pieces which we had hoped to include had been lost to the storm. Yet the walls of our gallery were crowded with evidence that the arts were alive and well in McClellanville. Several of the images from that show, which was curated by Jay Shuler and partially funded by the Trident Community Foundation Expansion Arts Fund, are included in this book.

The McClellanville Coast Cookbook is the work of many hands. The Board of Directors of the McClellanville Arts Council provided vision, advice, financial support, and much hard work. Bonnie Riedesel served as Director of the Arts Council in 1988-90, during our early exploration of local traditions. Folklorist Gail Matthews started us off on the right foot by conducting interviews and photographing local craftspeople. Ruth Middleton, Alison Reside, Billy Dinwiddie, and I conducted additional interviews. Alison spent hours tracking down recipes for local specialities--and typing them up. So did Robyn Dudley, who set the project rolling when she walked into our consignment shop and asked, "Where can I find information about the history and foodways of this area?" In the spring of 1992, the Arts Council asked students at McClellanville Middle School to interview their parents and grandparents about life in McClellanville; several of the resulting essays are quoted in this book. Dale Rosengarten copyedited and helped lay out the manuscript. Jenna McClellan, Jackie Morrison, Marylou High, Ellen Baxter, and Martha Zierden helped proofread.

Jeff Stivers taught me how to use my computer to typeset the book and rescued me from countless electronic crises. The McClellanville Telephone Company copied many a page for us and provided technical assistance.

Bernadette Humphrey did whatever needed to be done, whether it was soliciting recipes, photographing the mural for the cover, or making arrangements with the printer. I thank her for keeping her sense of humor--and helping me to keep mine.

Most of all, we thank those who talked with us about fishing, farming, and food; the artists and writers whose work appears in these pages; and the many McClellanville-area residents who submitted recipes. This book represents the beginning, not the end, of a journey. We invite our neighbors and friends to continue submitting recipes and reminiscences so that the next edition of *The McClellanville Coast Cookbook* will be even bigger and better.--**Susan Williams**

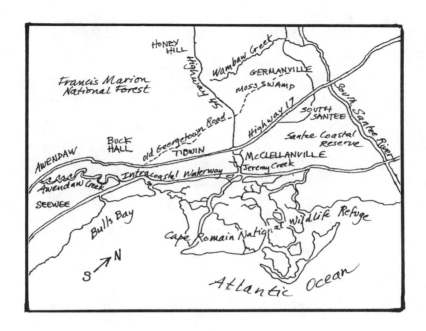

The McClellanville Coast

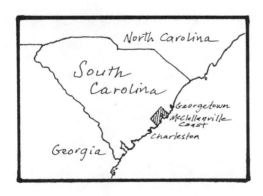

AWASH WITH FOOD
by Jay Shuler, Doe Hall

I remember crabs. At low tide, I would go bogging barefoot in Jeremy Creek, probing puddles and pools left behind by the ebbing water. There crabs waited for the tide's return. They buried themselves in the muck, all but invisible, showing only a hair-thin outline of the front of their shells and their stalked eyes. Easy to pin with a stick and pick up. I dropped them into a bucket. Every so often, one of the crabs would prove to be a "softy," good luck because Martha's grandfather would pay a dime for a "softy" and only fifteen cents for a dozen hard-shelled crabs. R.L. Morrison (everyone called him "Bah") was the village gourmand. My feet are still scarred from bogging among sharp oyster shells to find "softies" to satisfy his craving for crabs and mine for candy.

Among the items offered for a pittance at McClellanville doors were whiting and mullet, the latter still kicking when they reached our porch. Mullet must be eaten within a few hours of leaving the water, or they taste like any other fishy fish. Freshly netted shrimps, too, were offered, tiny creatures called "creek shrimp," difficult to shell, but wonderful for salad or pilau.

A fleet of small trawlers, operated by Portuguese fishermen, brought commercial shrimping to McClellanville in the mid-thirties. One of the fishermen, Joe Gumm, rented a room from us. Lonely for the family he left behind in Portugal, he treated me and my brother "Boots" as though he were a doting uncle. When shrimp were running, he bought us gifts. Once he gave us fine matching sheep-skin coats; another time, air-rifles.

Joe decided to treat us to a Portuguese delicacy-- stewed octopus. He caught two with arms about three feet long and told my mother they had to be dried before cooking. He hung them on a branch of the cedar tree within two feet of the kitchen window. He checked them when he came in from the sea, and after a few weeks he pronounced them almost ready--"Cook 'em tomorrow."

Next morning, my mother looked innocent and puzzled as we wondered out loud--who could have cut the cord and allowed the octopus to ruin on the sandy ground?

In addition to octopus, and in contrast to highly regarded oysters and clams, McClellanville palates scorned several seafoods others considered delicacies. As squid were worthless in the village, most shrimpers tossed them over the rail with the other "trash." A few shrimpers saved the squid they netted, and shipped them off to New York where they brought a good price. Mussels were not gathered commercially, but about 1940, McClellanville was under serious consideration for the site of a factory to extract vitamin D from them. The project was dropped when December 7, 1941, changed all of our plans.

From the swamp woods of summer came buckets of huckleberries, plucked at some risk from the lairs of cane-brake rattlesnakes. In fall and winter, deer were hunted. One or two were almost always hanging from a hook in the ceiling of our back hall, dripping blood caught by sheets of the *News and Courier* spread on the floor. My father was the premier turkey hunter of McClellanville. He made his own hand-size boxes of cedar, one side of which had a lip which when stroked by a thin bar of slate

Harvesting Sweet Potatoes, a woodcut by Dale Rosengarten.

produced a perfect imitation of a coy turkey hen. One week, my mother planned to serve turkey salad at her bridge club, but forgot to tell my father until the day before the meeting. He drove off in his Model A and within an hour returned with a gobbler.

My grandfather, R.T. Morrison ("Nine-finger Dick" because his five-year-old sister had playfully amputated his index finger when he was three) grew vegetables at Laurel Hill, the family place six miles south of the village on the oyster-shell-paved road to Charleston. He cultivated Irish potatoes, stringbeans, cucumbers, cantaloupe, watermelon, lettuce, and tomatoes for the New York market. The crisp white lettuce had to be packed in shaved ice, and a great machine in the packing shed piled up mountains of it. My first cousin Ted Dawson and I discovered that a fully ripened tomato buried about an arm's length in the ice would crystallize into a delicious crimson popsicle.

While my grandfather farmed two hundred acres, my grandmother tended an orchard in the yard producing pecans, walnuts, every imaginable kind of fig, and several varieties of grape. She always planted a garden across the road in which at least half of the rows were given over to zinnias and marigolds that in season ornamented her parlor. The vegetables in the other rows duplicated those in the fields, with the added delicacies of strawberries, logan berries, asparagus, and leeks.

We were awash with food in McClellanville.

FIFTEEN HEAD AT THE TABLE

An Interview with John Ackerman, Honey Hill

Mama cooked biscuits about three times a day, I think, and she'd have to cook about three panfuls to have enough to go around. I had two brothers and nine sisters.

Papa would go down to McClellanville for Christmas. That's the only place you could get anything. He'd borrow old man Ed Wilson's buggy, hitch the horse to the buggy, trot to McClellanville. Take him about two hours. Go down there and buy firecrackers, these little old cap pistols--50 cent for a pistol and a bunch of caps--fruit and stuff for them young'uns. You couldn't buy dollbabies or nothin' like that--you couldn't find none of them. He'd go by hisself, once a year. Buy coconuts, fruit, and stuff. Probably spend $5 or $10.

For Christmas my mother would cook at least seven or eight cakes, pies. Potato pies, plain cake, jelly cake, coconut cake. She'd take that old big coconut, break it open. She had an old grating thing she'd grate it on, make coconut pies and coconut cake. I've never seen such cakes in my life. I liked that jelly cake. She'd make them little thin layers, about seven or eight high. She'd make two or three of them 'cause it'd take that many to get a slice around.

Had our own rice, corn, meat, lard--all we had to buy was a little flour and sugar, coffee. The rest we raised ourselves.

My daddy never eat a nothin' in this world but hog meat, all of his life, and he lived to be 92 years old. Never had nothin' wrong with him-- never been in no hospital 'til he was 86 years old. Had all of his teeth, eyes didn't need no glasses. We killed anywhere from 35 to 45 hogs a year, salted them down. Try out the lard, put it in the can. We'd get them 48 lb. cans, set 'em in a #3 washtub, pour water in the tub. That's to keep that hot grease from melting that seam on them lard cans.

We'd kill six to eight hogs a day--that's about all you could take care of in one day 'cause you had to kill 'em, clean 'em, cut 'em up, salt 'em, cut up all the fat, put it in the washpot, cut all the lean meat off and grind it up for sausage--all that you had to do in one day. Smokehouse was four sides, a top, a dirt bottom. Spread a sack down on the dirt, salt that meat and put it right down on that sack.

We'd start butchering about September--kill a hog and eat it, kill another'n and eat it, start in November to salting 'em down on the dirt. Let it stay down three weeks, take it up, rework the joints. Isaac Green, he done all that--he'd take the hams, break the joints loose, work 'em like that, limber 'em back up, wash all the salt off 'em, put borax on 'em. Take this old beargrass, split a little hole in the skin. Had strips on top of the smokehouse, hang it up there. We never did smoke it. As soon as we got all that off the dirt--kill another batch. We eat a lot of meat, see.

People used to have hogs and cows--had a brand and a mark, and had them recorded in the courthouse in Moncks Corner. And every summer in May and June we penned the cows up, keep 'em up a month or two, kind of tame them cows--if you didn't you couldn't handle 'em. Brand the calves, turn 'em back in the woods--or sell 'em.

A lady in McClellanville, Beulah Sullivan, she used to butcher, and had a meat market across the street. She used to come butcher the cows herself. She'd tell the old man, says, "Pen me up a cow--I've got to have some beef." She'd come in, and wherever we had the cow, she'd shoot it down right there, butcher it right there, put it in the truck, carry it to McClellanville. She'd get that knife and *fall* on that cow, son.

We planted two acres of rice--had a big family-- and we got 84 bushels of clean rice (rough), the last year.we planted, sometime between 1932 and 1935. Eighty-four bushels lasted three years. The Wampee rice field was just the other side of that tower yonder. The little drain, called Briary drain--that spring keeps it running all the time. Them springs, they boil all the time in there. The old man was in charge of this field out here, the Wambaw. There was about ten head planting out there. I don't remember who was in charge of the Wampee rice field but I think some of these Wilsons were.

You couldn't plant one place every year. You'd go to a new place every year, so it would have some timber on it where you could burn it. That burning killed all the undergrowth, see, killed all the sprouts, weeds, and everything. Bushes ten or twelve feet high were best to burn--myrtle bushes, sweet gum bushes, some pine. They'd get *hot.* Ten or twelve families would get together and plant a big field.

It's a spring in there in the old rice field. In slavery times they built banks around their spring--they called it a reserve. They'd have it cut off in little banks all over the rice field. They'd take two cedar logs and drop them on top of the bank like that. Then they'd dig from under them logs out and then they'd stick boards down in there--that was the gate, to hold in the water. They cut the trees down, everything in the area--take about five people to cut five acres. They'd let it die down a little bit, wilt, you know, and then they'd go in there and burn it. This was in the summertime, spring, around May.

Then they'd open that gate there, and shut the back one, and flood it with water. Maybe some places be twelve inches deep, some places four or five. Did that to kill all the morning glories and all that, after that fire burned over, see. The fire burned up all the limbs and stuff but it wouldn't burn the logs. They'd be laying there all over the place. But that didn't affect the rice, you know. And then they'd go in there and sow the seed, right in the water, broadcast it, you know. I've seen some of them colored women throw a bushel of rough rice on their head and walk from here to the rice field. They had one man to do all the sowing--old Isaac Green--because he knew how to regulate it. In that water you couldn't see it. We'd be sowing about the last of May. We planted Blue Ribbon rice--bought the seed. The old man tried to keep some seed from one year to the next, for seed, but it didn't come up too good.

You let that water stay on it until you could see it sprouting little white roots. You could look in the shallow water and see 'em. Then you open the back gate just a little bit--not much. You didn't want it to wash all the seeds out, just gradually go down. Then those seeds would get more attached to the dirt--wouldn't be floating, like. And they'd take root in three or four days. Then the heads bust open and the green start sprouting out. Them old colored people took care of all the water, see. They was old when we was boys. They'd planted rice before. One fellow took care of all the water--Oliver Wilson. He'd lived right out here since slavery.

Soon as things got sprouted up about a inch they turned the water back on it and it'd grow right up in that water, get up two or three inches high and they'd turn the water back off of it--slowly, you know, 'til it was mostly dry. And they didn't turn the water back on it but one more time, when it got up about a foot high. And after a couple of days they'd turn it back. That was to kill all the weeds and stuff. Then it would *grow*. You didn't have to bother it no more--just let it grow itself. It'd get up about three feet high and start putting on heads, about the middle of June.

The only thing you had to worry about then was the birds--they're called Maybirds, them blackbirds. The hen would be brown, sort of, and the rooster *black*. You couldn't see the dirt for 'em, there were so many. They'd fly in there, perch, and pick that seed. It was like milk in there, and they'd suck that milk, and that seed wouldn't be no good. So you had to mind the birds out of there until it started to getting hard. Walk around there, shoot the gun off, and keep them off. Couldn't shoot 'em on dirt--you'd shoot all the heads off the rice. Had to shoot 'em in the air. We took turns, for about two weeks. It took about two weeks for that head to get hard, and soon as it got hard they wouldn't bother it.

Start drying up, turning gold color. Soon as it got dry enough they'd go in there and cut it with a reef hook. You'd take the reef hook and catch a bundle in your hand, then reach down and cut it with the reef hook, take a couple of straws and wrap around to tie it, lay it down. Soon as you got it cut, then you had to stack it.

You'd stand that bundle straight up, put there, put there, put there, put there. You'd get the heads to locking together, and they'd hold it up, see. You get a stack about eight feet in diameter, one layer high, then you'd come back and stand off on the side, lay three or four bundles right in the center to make it higher, then take another bundle and come down, like a housetop. And you'd go all the way around like that, 'til you got as high as you could reach. Six, seven foot high. That's a stack. You could leave it in the field and it wouldn't get wet--the rain would run off of it.

Then whenever you got time you'd sew six or seven old crocus bags together to make a burlap sheet, lay it out on the dirt. White people didn't do much threshing--colored women did that, mostly. They'd take a hoe handle about six feet long, cut a groove in the top, tie a piece of rawhide from this one to that one. That's what they'd thrash it out with. Lay a stack here with the heads. Beat it off, beat it off. Thirty-five or forty bundles at one time. Beat the heads off the straw. We'd have eight or nine stacks off an acre, and one woman could thrash off a whole stack in one day by herself. Them colored women would get out there and start atalkin' and alaughin' and asingin', and beatin' them things. *Boom, te boom, te boom, te boom.* They had a rhythm with it, boy. They'd throw that pole over this side they shoulder one time and over that side one time. *Bam a bam a bam a bam.* That thing would hit that dirt just as smooth as could be. It wouldn't bounce. They'd wear them things out, now. Beat it off, beat it off, beat it off. Keep pushing the straw off.

Take all the straw off the burlap, fold up the burlap, and pour the rough rice in a sack. Then they had what they called a rice fan, pour it in there, and this thing had a handle on it and blades in there that turn fast, blow all them little broken up pieces of straw and stuff out of there. You could take something and fan the rice by hand, but that was too slow. We had one machine and everybody used it.

Put the rough rice in the barn in a bin and just leave it until you want to carry some to the mill and have it chafted, we call it--take the chaff off of it. When you carry it to the mill, you could carry a bushel of rough rice and get anywhere from fourteen to sixteen quarts of white rice. Take the chaff and give it to the hogs. They'd take two quarts of your rice for milling a bushel. The mill was at the store, Hubert Shuler's store. Take the horse, wagon, put two bushel of corn in there and a bushel of rice, go to the mill every other week. Grind a bushel of it half and half--half meal and half grits. That's for us. And a bushel, all meal, for the dogs.

That rice got a lot more starch in it than rice you buy in the store nowadays. It was good, sweet-like. Some people said they didn't like it. But I loved it. But that's all we was raised on. Fifteen head sat down at our table every meal-- they could eat up some rice, now.

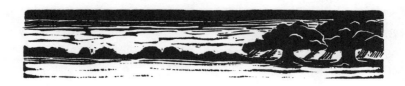

FISHING AND FARMING
An Interview with Elizabeth Colleton, Tibwin

When your daddy is a fisherman, you're going to come in contact with a lot of fish. I don't like mullet fish up to this day, because it seemed like mullet was the only fish in the creek. They could catch it by the tubful. They would string it with a plant that grows on the seashore, green, with a white flower, something like a cactus. String it through the gills. It's really tough, you know. They tie that, put so many and so many fish on it, go round and sell it. Sold it by the string.

There was not too much of money, so what they did--they swap. You carry the fish, and if they didn't have the money for the fish maybe they had some cornmeal, maybe they had some sugar, some eggs. My daddy made his own boat. He used to make boats for most of the other fishermen, too, and the oars, and the nets. He had one, called the mullet net, and one for shrimp, too. One was more coarse, when they weave it.

He used to weave the baskets, too, real big baskets. They used to use them to fan the rice. When you finish beating your rice and you want to get all that chaff out the rice, you have to have a fanner. Those baskets were going for $1, $1.50 for the big ones. His nets would sell for $1. As time went on he got $2. That's just how he survived. He kept on making those things until he started supervising the sawmill for the Loftons when Mr. Lofton was a state representative. My daddy carried on the whole business. He had a fifth grade education but I bet you couldn't beat him figuring.

When we go crabbing, we bogged. Go down in the creek, in the little streams. We took our pails and we picked up our crabs. When the tide goes down the crabs are in their little bed--you can see them. You put that stick over those two fins and you take that back part, pick it up. When we see the female and the male together we would always say, "There goes Old Mole and his wife." We used to call the bigger crab Old Mole and the smaller his wife, when we met them together.

The river was really ours. And you didn't hear about children drowning out there, either. They learned how to protect themselves. We went out in that deep water--we'd pick oysters, we'd catch crabs. Sometimes we go out there at night with my brothers. That's when you'd catch most of your mullet fish.

You'd see the porpoise all just running the school of fish. The fish want to run away from the porpoise, and they'll go up in these little streams. My brothers would put their boat up to the end of that stream, throw out that net over there, and catch a net full of fish. The porpoise going to stay in the big stream, and when they come by, the little fish want to get away.

The Singletons had two raw houses right there in Tibwin. That's where they open the raw oysters. In Buck Hall they had the steam oyster factory--that's Shellmore. They were the big factory that canned oysters, and they canned okra and tomato in the summer. Most of the farmers around here would send their okra and tomato and mustard and other vegetables, because the same factory that did oysters in the winter did vegetables in the summer. They employed a lot of people to the oyster factory. I worked in the vegetables--I never worked in the oysters, I was too young. My mother and sisters worked in the oysters.

I peeled the tomatoes. They'd plunge them into hot water; then they had a tray, and this would roll on down on a chain. There was a line of us. You could stop it as it rolled. What's left-- that's what they make the juice out of. When they got a shucker for the oysters, that's when the employment went. That machine could do more work than forty or fifty employees.

They used to sell the oyster shell to the highway department because back then the roads were unpaved. They had a machine to crush it. Some of that shell they take back in the river and plant it for another crop of oysters. They have to put so much back in the river so they can have the reproduction of oysters.

My father started doing truck farming for the Loftons in the late thirties. On the farm then they grew white potatoes, tomatoes, string beans, cut turnips. He even grew peanuts a couple of years, watermelon, things like that. We would have to pick the bugs off the tomatoes, put 'em in a cup of kerosene. Each one of us had a little cup. It was mostly the young children would do that, while the older ones did the hoeing. At that time there wasn't tractors. Later on they started with pesticide. They would have a crocus bag and they would cut that into squares and they would put a couple of quarts of that pesticide in there. Then you'd shake it--you'd go down the row and shake it on. It wasn't until the late fifties that they had a machine that would go down the row and spray it on two sides.

During that time we had a garden year 'round. Back then they had their garden fenced in, secured. It wasn't wire fence--they would call it clapboard; these were drilled out of the trees out of the woods. You would have vegetables from that garden the whole year 'round. They would plant a summer crop and they would plant a fall crop.

Hoover times were really hard, really tough for most people, but then when Roosevelt took the seat, he gave them seed. Before then, we would save the seed. You save your peanut seed, you save your corn seed and your okra seed--you save everything that you plant, even the collard greens. They would let that seed dry, and they would thrash it off, and then they would secure that for the next season. There were no seed stores. And they really lived off the farm.

They say a lot of Indians used to live in Shulerville and some of those areas. Some of my late ancestors were of that Indian descent, on my grandmother's side and my grandfather's. Some was from that Twelve Mile area. That's how they learned to plant the farm--you know the Indians were the first ones planting corn, that sort of thing.

We grew our own rice. To thrash it they had two long sticks, and they would tie that together. You see that wheeling--you would wheel it around, thrash that rice. In the fall you lay it out on a long canvas thing, and thrash it out--the rice would go on that. They used to take that straw from that rice and they used it to make their mattresses, pillows. My mother used to do that. They used every part of it.

Every family had a mortar and pestle. My daddy would get the cedar--some people had it out of the big pine but the cedar and oak would last longer. He hew out that center, and when he finish it look like a bowl. The rice never would come real white, but they would take the cornshuck and put it in there and beat that with the rice to get it white. They say that whited it--it would sand it off a little, and it wouldn't be as red.

My daddy had a long sift; he made it out of wire. That's how you separate the corn meal and the grits from the hucks. A corn has three departments--it has the hucks, then it has the grits, and it has the meal. When you put them in this big sift, that takes out all the grits and the meal. Then you have your hucks--that, you feed to the hogs. Then you have a smaller sift and then you have to sift it again--then you got your meal, and what's left in your sift is your grits.

We had one mill in Buck Hall, run by Mr. Taffy Cash--he had the sugarcane mill too. After his death, his son--his name is Stephanie Cash--started operating it. Then the Dawseys, they had a mill. You had two-three places to go. Mr. Claudee was the first one really that had a mill that would pound the rice. Then your rice would come out nice and white.

We also planted "benne"--now they call it sesame seeds. Benne seed is just a seed like collard seed or rape, mustard. They're small like that but they're little and white. The plant got little beans on it. When they grow, they pop--little seeds inside. Cut them down, put them in a crocus bag, hang 'em up, and they'd drop down in that sack. You take your syrup and you make benne candy just like you make peanut candy. The plantations planted benne for the birds--they'd have little feeders out in the woods for the doves and the quails. Millionaires--they would have little fields all over for the deer, and the birds. They would have millets, bennes--now they have what you call lespedeza.

Everybody had hogs. That's how you get your meat. That mostly came in the fall, when you finish with harvesting, around November. They'd make sausage, cut it up in ham, pork chops. Then they'd cure it.

They'd make hogshead cheese. That's real nice. You clean the head, take that meat and cut it up. You have a meat grinder, you just cook that meat enough to get it off the bones and then throw in a little bit more lean in it. We used to trim a little of the fat.

We'd always save the sack from the flour you buy at the store, bleach it good, and have that sack nice and white. We put all that meat in that bag, put it back in a pot of broiling water, and let it broil. And then when we finish we had a strainer--we set that over and let it drain. We put onion, black pepper, seasoning in it. Pack it, press it, put it in a pan, let it cool. Cut it in chunks. I used to like it on hominy grits.

They used that same grinder to do the sausage. Cut some of the lean, some of the fat. Season it. Everybody couldn't do the sausage. My mother could--she used to work for the Loftons. The Loftons raised a lot of hogs, and they had what you call a stuffer. It was a machine, but it was used by hand. They used the hog intestine, the small one. To get that intestine where it'd be thin, you have to scrape off all that fat. It becomes real thin, like a balloon.

This was one thing I hated, when you had to blow it up to see if it's thin enough. I didn't like that part. My mother used to do all that for the Loftons when they kill the hogs, nine or ten at one time. They have to clean all those chitlins. Her job was to scrape them. And then they put them in a big jar of salt water, and the next day they start stuffing. That was the most delicious sausage.

Back then they never barbecued much. Everything was cooked on that nice wood stove. We had an old man from Germanville, grew up on the Rutledge plantation. Used to call him "Babaloo"--I think his name was Louis Colleton. He was really good on barbecue.

We kept cows, but our cows was for paying tax. That cow would have a calf, and they would raise that calf, and that calf was the money to pay that tax. That's what my mama and my grandmama and all of them did. They all had cows, and that calf gonna be paying that tax. We'd eat beef from the market, but I never saw my family kill a cow. They'd sell it to Mr. Solomon or Mr. Sutler and they'd do the butchering. They had the markets and that's how we got our beef.

My daddy used to trap raccoon--now that used to be delicious. Squirrels, rabbits, possum--man, that old possum is good baked down. My mama would bake hers, parboil it and put it in that stove and bake it 'til it's brown. I used to love that coon. When my kids were coming up I baked it. The coon is very good and lean. If you get a good leany one, it's real nice. But they'd eat up all your green corn and your watermelons.

My mother had eight of us--six girls and two boys. We were always trained to do everything on the farm, and we were happy. As children we were really happy. Our parents put food on the table and clothes on our backs, and we were happy.

Tomatoes, a photograph by Bernadette Humphrey.

Fisherman's Choice, a painting by Richard Hume Lucas (1825-1915), courtesy of Peter Manigault.

SEAFOOD

I've watched the shrimping industry here from when everything was done by hand until now everything is done by computer. Navigation is all done by computers, all the work is done by hydraulics and machinery, and you can take a person today that doesn't know a thing in the world about fishing, show him a computer and set his rig for him, and he can go fishing and do well--or at least they think they can. Years ago when we first started out everything was done with your eyes. Navigation was done from looking at objects on the land, or as some of the fellows said, when you got forty or fifty miles off shore the better fishermen could look in the try net and see the bottom samples and tell you where they were from the shells and the bottom debris.

Sonny Morrison

SOUL GUMBO

Few slices of bacon
1 cup ham chunks, diced
1 lb. Kielbasa Polish sausage
2 lbs. chicken wingettes
1 cup onions
3 cloves garlic
1 cup celery
2 cups carrots
1½ lbs. raw medium shrimp
2½ dozen live blue crabs
1 lb. scallops
1 pt. oysters
1 lb. halibut
2 quart cans tomatoes
1½ lbs. fresh or frozen okra
Salt and pepper to taste
3 bay leaves

Peel and clean shrimps. If you use baby scallops leave whole. If you use regular size scallops, cut them in four pieces. Do not wash oysters. (Check for shell pieces and grit.) Clean crabs while still raw. Leave legs and claws on body. Leave yellow stuff in crabs. Break in half. If you cannot find halibut (or if it's too expensive) use a fish that has firm flesh that will not crumble when cooked.

Now you are ready to create a dish that will make you kick the dog when it's all gone. Cut bacon in pieces; fry in a large pot. Remove bacon (do not eat or throw away). Add diced ham, sliced sausage, and chicken wingettes. Cook until half done, turning constantly (almost stirring). Add chopped onions, diced garlic, and diced celery; cook until onions are translucent. Toss around in pot (not a complete stirring motion). Add carrots and cook five minutes more. Add shrimp, crabs, scallops, oysters, halibut, and okra. Toss around in pot for about five minutes. Add tomatoes, salt and pepper to taste, and bay leaves. Please do not overcook. Turn up heat on stove. Let come to a rolling boil for 1 minute. Turn off heat and let stand for a few minutes (maybe 10 minutes). Serve over a scoop of rice. Put a basket of hot garlic bread on the table and watch your family or guests beg for more.

Dorothy Talley

NO-GENDER CRAB STEW
OR "SAVE THE SHE-CRABS"

¼ cup finely chopped onion
2 Tbs. butter
1 lb. flaked crab meat
2 Tbs. flour
4 cups milk
1 cup cream
1 cup cooked corn
1 cup cooked, small lima beans
1 tsp. Worcestershire sauce
Salt
Pepper
4 Tbs. dry sherry
3 hard-boiled egg yolks

Simmer onions in butter until tender. Add crabmeat and heat thoroughly. Add flour, milk, and cream, and cook, stirring, until thick. Now add the corn, lima beans, and Worcestershire sauce. Season to taste. Just before serving add the sherry and crumble ½ of an egg yolk in the bottom of each bowl or cup. Serves 6.

Adam Howard

TREASURE OF THE KITCHEN
SHRIMP SOUP

The French call any juices "The Treasure of the Kitchen." Never throw them away. The most delicious flavor of shrimps is the fat between the head and body, so if shrimp are cooked fresh, the heads should be left on.

Juice from sautéed shrimp (with heads on)
1 Tbs. lemon juice
1 pint chicken broth
1 pint half-and-half
Dash Worcestershire sauce
Dash mace
Salt and pepper to taste
Handful of fresh mushrooms, sliced
½ cup thinly sliced celery
¼ cup onions (optional)
4 Tbs. butter

Save the juice from 1 pound (or more) sautéed shrimp. Sauté celery, mushrooms, and onions briefly in butter. Add rest of the ingredients and bring just to simmer. Garnish with shrimps or parsley or paprika or chives. Add more ingredients for more people and experiment with the amounts to your taste. Serves 4.

Martha Shuler

MOSS SWAMP CATFISH STEW

5 lbs. catfish, cleaned
5 lbs. peeled potatoes
3 lbs. chopped onions
5 lbs. whole peeled tomatoes
1 Tbs. fine black pepper
Cayenne pepper

Boil catfish and pick meat from bones. Save 1 quart of juice. Boil potatoes and onions for 30 minutes in ½ gallon water. Add tomatoes, fish, cayenne and black pepper, and salt to taste. Add 1 quart fish juice. Cook on low heat for 4 hours, stirring frequently to avoid sticking and to break up ingredients into a sort of mush. Feeds 10 hungry beer drinkers--men or women. A great winter-time pick-me-up.

Dan Wheeler

EASY SOUTHERN CATFISH STEW
OR MEDITERRANEAN FISH SOUP

2 cans sliced stewed tomatoes (Mexican or Italian)
1 or 2 cans of water, depending on how thick you like your soup
1 large potato, peeled and diced
1 large onion, thinly sliced
1 lb. fish filet, any kind
Optional--1 or 2 cubes fish boullion if you really want your stew to taste fishy; 1 or 2 dashes of Hot Pete sauce for southern catfish stew.

Put all ingredients in a pot. Bring to a boil, then let simmer 15 minutes and serve. You'll have to work a lot harder to make a better stew (or soup) from scratch.

Walter Bonner

NEW ENGLAND SPOT TAIL CHOWDER

½ lb. bacon, cooked and crumbled
4 medium potatoes, diced and cooked
2 small onions, chopped
Salt
Freshly ground pepper
1 quart half-and-half
2 cups spot tail bass, uncooked, cut into chunks

Cook bacon, drain and crumble. Sauté onions in small amount of bacon grease. In a large pot combine bacon, onions, potatoes, half-and-half, milk, salt, and pepper. Bring to a low boil, stirring constantly so chowder won't burn. Add the Spot Tail Bass and cook at a low temperature until the fish is done. Serves 8-10 people. Chowder is best the next day after the flavors have blended.

Marylou High

SHRIMP AND CORN CHOWDER

1 lb. peeled and cleaned shrimp
2 cans cream-style corn
4 medium potatoes, diced and cooked
2 medium onions, chopped
Salt and freshly ground pepper
1 quart half-and-half
Butter or margarine

In a separate pan sauté onions in butter or margarine. In a large pot combine onions, cream-style corn, potatoes, half-and-half, milk, and salt and pepper. Bring to a low boil, stirring constantly so it won't burn. Add shrimp and cook at a low temperature until shrimp are pink. Serves 8-10 people.

This chowder is best the next day, after the flavors have blended.

Marylou High

"ALLERGIC TO CLAMS" CHOWDER

I cannot eat clams or oysters due to an allergy, but everyone loves my clam chowder and oyster stew. So I make up this recipe without tasting it, strictly by smell. I always make up a big pot and freeze what isn't eaten for later.

Steam clams in a deep kettle. Be sure to retain the liquor for the chowder. Slice about ½ lb. bacon into small bits. Fry bacon in deep kettle (do not drain bacon grease). As the bacon is browning add onion, cut up in small pieces. Add garlic, salt, pepper, celery (salt or fresh), or anything else you'd like. Pour liquor from clams into kettle. Add 5 or 6 potatoes (diced, sliced, chopped, or however) to the kettle. Boil until tender. The clams can be chopped with a knife if desired but I usually run them through the food processor or blender. After potatoes are tender, add about 2 cups of milk, then add the clams. If you like your chowder thicker add some instant mashed potatoes to the broth.

Maggi Yergin

OYSTER-ASPARAGUS SOUP

1 (16 oz.) can white asparagus (drain and add ice water)
1 (16 oz.) pkg. frozen green asparagus (save tips and chop stems)
1 cup oysters (chop and save juice)
2 cups dry white wine
2 Tbs. butter
2 cups whipping cream
10 oz. chicken stock
Flour
Salt
Black pepper

Boil white wine and add oysters slowly. When all are added turn down and simmer for one minute, then turn off, keep covered, and set aside. In saucepan melt butter; add 1 cup cream and make sauce with flour. Thin with chicken broth, added slowly and stirred in. Turn burner up to medium heat. Add chopped asparagus and then oyster broth (save out oysters). Bring rapidly to a boil, quickly add oysters and chilled asparagus tips, and serve.

Billy Dinwiddie

SAND DUNE SURPRISE

First you need a boat to get you to the islands, and lots of friends to do the collecting. Send your friends out to collect any type of live shell fish (conchs, pen shells, cockles, oysters, crabs, etc.) Meanwhile, start a nice fire and get some sea water boiling to cook the critters in. After the basic stock is done, pour some of it off into a separate container and throw the rest away. Add to the stock cans of mushroom soup, celery soup, cream of chicken soup, or any other you desire. Add chopped-up critter bodies to the kettle and cook until hot. This recipe is best in the winter when everyone is really hungry. They'll eat anything then!

Maggi Yergin

Lee Arthur

CRAB POT CRAB CAKES

1 lb. crab, clean and white meat
20 Captain's wafers, crumbled
½ onion, chopped
¼ bell pepper, chopped
¼ cup evaporated milk
Worcestershire sauce
Mustard

Sauté onion and bell pepper; combine with crabmeat, crumbs, and Worcestershire. Add evaporated milk and mix again. Add a touch of mustard. Form into cakes and grill, or put mixture into crab shells.

Laura McClellan, The Crab Pot Restaurant

CRAB CAKES

1 lb. special crabmeat
1 egg white
1 Tbs. fresh lime juice
2 Tbs. mayonnaise
½ cup freshly ground cracker crumbs
Salt
Fresh ground pepper

Combine above ingredients in a medium-size bowl. Mixture should be easy to handle and not too sticky. Form into patties and roll in a reserve of freshly ground cracker crumbs. Sauté on medium heat in butter or margarine. Makes 12 medium cakes; will serve 6.

Marylou High

Marie Sanders picks crabs at the South Carolina
Crab Company, a photograph by Wade Spees.

HOT CRAB-SHRIMP SPREAD

1 lb. shrimp, peeled, cooked, and chopped
1 cup crab meat (½ lb.)
1 medium onion, chopped fine
8 Tbs. butter
4 Tbs. flour (plain)
1 Tbs. Worcestershire sauce
1 tsp. dry mustard
½ cup evaporated milk
¼ cup grated Parmesan cheese
1 can sliced water chestnuts, chopped
1 cup mayonnaise
1 cup sour cream
¼ cup lemon juice

Melt 4 Tbs. butter in skillet. Sauté onion 'til limp, add shrimp and crab meat. Set aside. In separate saucepan melt remaining butter and stir in flour, making a paste. Add Worcestershire, mustard, and milk 'til blended. Combine with shrimp and crab. Preheat oven to 300 degrees. In separate bowl combine remaining ingredients and add to shrimp and crab mixture. Pour into lightly greased casserole dish and bake 30 minutes. Good with ½ cup toasted chopped or slivered almonds on top. This dish may be made a day ahead and refrigerated, but you should then increase the baking time by 15 minutes.
Sherry Browne

CRAB DIP

8 oz. carton sour cream
3 oz. cream cheese, softened
3 Tbs. mayonnaise
1 package dry Italian dressing mix
Squeeze of lemon
Grated cheddar cheese (however much you like)
¼ lb. crab meat

Mix first 3 ingredients together, then add other ingredients. Make sure you pick crab meat real good.

I've probably had this recipe for about ten years. A really good friend gave it to me. It was her mother's recipe--she was the one who concocted it. The thing that makes this recipe really good is the Italian Dressing mix--it has plenty of seasoning to add zest.

Carolyn Page

May at the Crab Pot, a silhouette by Clay Rice, courtesy of Laura McClellan.

Willie May Kilgore
August 27, 1939--July 19, 1992

She could cook anything. I really loved anything she fixed because she really fixed it good. All of her cooking was good.

She was just as sweet and loving a person--she loved to make other people happy. You'll never find another person like that--never.
Artha Mae Lewis

CRAB POT CRAB DIP

1 pint sour cream
1 lb. fresh crabmeat (claw and white)
1 tsp. Worcestershire sauce
Lemon juice to taste
1 tsp. horseradish
A dab of mayonnaise
⅓ cup sharp cheddar, grated
Cracker crumbs to add texture
A dab of cocktail sauce

Mix together and serve with crackers.

Laura McClellan, The Crab Pot Restaurant

SHRIMP DUFFY

1-2 lbs. shrimp, peeled
1 stick of butter
6 cloves of garlic, mashed
Juice of 1 lemon
½ can of beer (preferably Budweiser)
Chopped parsley
Salt to taste
Generous sprinkling of cayenne pepper

Melt butter in pan. Sauté garlic. Add shrimp until pink. Add lemon juice, beer, salt, parsley, and pepper. Reduce heat, cover, and cook 15 minutes. Serve over hot rice.

This recipe was devised by a friend of ours from California--Jim Duffy. The recipe we were using called for white wine, which we didn't have. Jim substituted some of Donny's Budweiser, which we had plenty of. The result was fantastic. It's just about the only way we fix shrimp anymore.

Bonnie Riedesel

SHRIMP MARSEILLES

Pour several tablespoons of olive oil in a wok. When wok is very hot, sauté several handfuls of fresh shrimp with heads on. Add any herbs you want and a clove or two of crushed garlic, then stir until shrimp are crisp and pink. Add salt and pepper, Worcestershire sauce, and mace to taste. Serve on newspaper. Remove heads and suck and chew on them. Then peel and eat shrimps with good beer or wine. Delicious! Serve with a wedge of lemon or lime if desired.

Martha Shuler

Today in gala celebration,
Our little fleet was blest.
That harvest, that wondrous crustacean,
The lowly shrimp, no less.
    . . . .
In blessing the pursuing fleet,
Alas, we do not skimp.
And this is well, the truth to tell,
But who will bless the shrimp?

J.O. McClellan, from "Who Will Bless the Shrimp?"

COCONUT SHRIMP

1 lb. large shrimp
¼ cup flour
½ tsp. salt
½ tsp. dry mustard
1 egg
2 Tbs. cream of coconut
⅓ cup bread crumbs
⅓ cup flaked coconut
3-4 cups vegetable oil

Peel and butterfly shrimp. Pour oil in 3" deep pan. Heat to 350 degrees. Combine flour, salt, and mustard in one bowl. Beat eggs and cream of coconut in another. In a third bowl mix coconut and breadcrumbs. Dip shrimp in flour mix, then egg mix, then breadcrumb mix. Fry shrimp 1½-2 minutes. Serve with Chinese Mustard Sauce.

Chinese Mustard Sauce

1 Tbs. dry mustard
⅓ cup honey
2 tsp. vinegar
¼ cup water

Mix well and keep cool.

Ellen Saum, Jeremy Creek Café

CURRIED SHRIMP

¼ cup butter or margarine
¼ cup onion, chopped
⅓ cup flour
1 tsp. salt
3 tsp. curry powder
1 cup chicken stock
2 cups milk
1 tsp. lemon juice
4 cups cooked shrimp

Melt butter; add onion and cook until tender. Stir in flour and seasonings, add stock, and cook until thick, stirring constantly. Add milk, lemon juice, and shrimp. Heat thoroughly. Serves 8.

Louise Leland Stroman

In McClellanville you can work as a shrimperman, because we live close to the ocean.

William Deas
McClellanville Middle School

Local legend has it that when the Seewee Indians complained to English settlers about conditions in the area, the settlers pointed out across the water and suggested that they should negotiate a treaty with the Queen. Finally the Indians got into their canoes and set out to find the Queen. Some were drowned, and the rest were sold into slavery. That was the end of the Seewee nation, or so the story goes.

SEEWEE SHRIMP

This recipe was left to an early planter of the Seewee region and has been passed through many generations of his family.

Any amount of shrimp may be steamed by this method. With help I have cooked as many as 100 lbs. for a church supper. Put in the washed shrimp and just enough water to cover the bottom of the pot. Add ½ to 1 tsp. of salt per lb. of shrimp, according to your taste. Then add nothing more than a few slices of onion, green pepper, or celery--no packet of seafood flavoring, no corn, and surely no sausage. Why adulterate nature's greatest seafood gift?

Turn on high heat and stand in front of the stove with one hand lifting the pot lid frequently and the other stirring the shrimp with a slotted spoon to keep them cooking in a uniform fashion. As the pan heats up, the shrimp making contact with the bottom will begin to turn pink first. Keep stirring every 30 seconds or so. Soon the water will boil and steam will appear. Rather suddenly--within minutes--the properly stirred shrimp will be uniformly pink. At that time a light froth will be evident in the pan, indicating that proteins from the cooked shrimp have escaped into the water. The shrimp are literally cooking in their own juice. You will be able to see that the flesh of some shrimp have separated slightly from their shells.

Dump the shrimp into a colander and shake them or stir them about to quickly cool them to room temperature. The stock can be saved for use in other seafood recipes. I like to serve the shrimp right after they are cooked. Let the diners pick the shells off themselves. For most occasions you will need to cook about ⅓ lb. of headed shrimp per person. If you expect to feed big eaters, put out about ⅔ lb. per person.

Walter Bonner

SHRIMP CREOLE

1 lb. fresh cleaned shrimp
½ cup green pepper, chopped
1 cup onion, chopped
4 slices bacon
1 (14 oz.) can Hunt's whole tomatoes, chopped
1 (14 oz.) can Hunt's tomato sauce
3 Tbs. Worcestershire sauce
6 drops Tabasco
½ tsp. black pepper
½ tsp. salt
3 or 4 bay leaves
2 tsp. sugar

Dry shrimp on paper towels. Fry bacon and remove from drippings. Sauté pepper and onion in bacon drippings; add tomatoes, tomato sauce, and seasonings. Simmer uncovered for 1 hour. Shortly before serving, add shrimp. Serve over hot rice. Top with crumbled bacon. Freezes well. More Worcestershire, Tabasco, and black pepper may be added for a hotter sauce.

Jo Luquire

SHRIMP IN BROWN GRAVY

Brown 2 or 3 slices salted butts meat. Sauté a small chopped onion and ½ small bell pepper in the drippings. Add 2 Tbs. flour and stir. Add 2 cups water and ½ tsp. Kitchen Bouquet. Stir over medium heat until thickened like gravy. Add 1 lb. peeled medium shrimp, deveined if necessary. Salt and pepper to taste. Serve over hot rice.

Debbie Thames

STEAMED CRABS

2 dozen crabs
Vinegar
2-3 jalapeño peppers, chopped

Put 1" liquid--half water, half vinegar--in bottom of large pot. Clean the crabs live by pulling off the back shells. Rinse. Crabs can then be refrigerated until ready for use. Put salt and pepper to taste on the crabs. Drop 2 or 3 jalapeño peppers onto crabs in pot, and steam for 20-30 minutes.

Betsey Hansen

CRAB-STUFFED POTATOES

12 large baking potatoes
1 cup butter or margarine, melted
1 cup milk
1 tsp. salt
½ tsp. freshly ground black pepper
2 bunches green onions
1 lb. lump crab meat, flaked
½ cup mayonnaise
½ cup sour cream
¼ cup fresh lemon juice
¼ tsp. ground red pepper
½ lb. bacon, cooked and crumbled

Preheat oven to 350 degrees. Prick potatoes all over with fork and place on jelly roll pan. Bake 1¼ to 1½ hours until tender when pricked. Remove from oven and cut in half lengthwise. Scoop out center. Leave ¼" thick shell. Beat potato in mixing bowl with sour cream, butter, salt, and pepper. Mix in crab meat, mayonnaise, and lemon juice. Stuff potato shells. Bake at 350 degrees for 40 to 45 minutes. Sprinkle bacon on top. Makes about 24 servings.

Lillian Duke

LOW COUNTRY SHERRIED SEAFOOD

2 lbs. shrimp, cooked and peeled
1 lb. claw crab meat
2 stalks celery, thinly sliced
1 medium bell pepper, chopped
1 medium onion, chopped
4 Tbs. butter or margarine
4 Tbs. flour
2 cups cream, milk, or canned milk
1 cup grated sharp cheddar cheese
Pinch of mace or dash of nutmeg
½ tsp. salt
⅛ tsp. pepper
½ cup cream (not cooking) sherry
½ to 1 cup cracker crumbs

Preheat oven to 400 degrees. Simmer celery, onion, and bell pepper in 2 cups water until tender and drain well. Melt butter in heavy skillet. Add flour, stirring until smooth. Slowly add cream, stirring constantly. Cook until thick. Stir in cheese, seasonings, and sherry. Remove from heat. Add drained vegetables to cream sauce. Gently stir in seafood. Place in greased 2-quart casserole. Top with crumbs and sprinkle with paprika. Bake 20 or 30 minutes or until browned and bubbly.
Cindy Buscemi

PAULA'S CREEK FOOD

2 pkgs. yellow rice (cook as directed)
1 lb. shrimp
1 lb. crabmeat
1 onion, chopped
1 bell pepper, chopped
1 Tbs. Worcestershire sauce
1 stick butter

Sauté seafood and vegetables in butter. Add Worcestershire sauce. Stir into rice and cook a few more minutes.

Paula Gooch

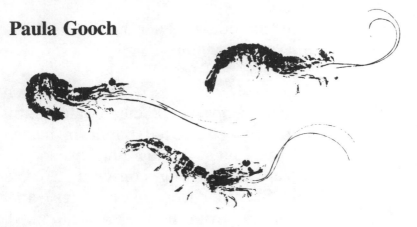

McClellanville is known for its big shrimp trawlers and good tasting shrimp.

Leroy Vann
McClellanville Middle School

OYSTER CASSEROLE

3 rolls Ritz crackers, crushed
2 pints shucked oysters with juice
1 stick butter
Tabasco sauce
Worcestershire sauce
1 egg
1 ¼ cups milk

Cover bottom of 9" round casserole dish with one roll of crushed crackers. Arrange layer of oysters on crackers, then dot with butter, Worcestershire sauce, and hot sauce. Repeat with a second layer of crackers, oysters, butter, and seasoning sauces. Top with cracker crumbs. Beat egg and milk; pour over casserole. Dot with butter and bake at 375 degrees until mixture is firm and top is crisp (approximately 45 minutes).

Mary Scott

RED SNAPPER
IN PARCHMENT PAPER

Have ready 4 portions of snapper filets, brushed with olive oil and sprinkled with a little salt and pepper. Make up a mixture of:
  Crumbled feta cheese
  Sliced black olives
  Chopped red onion
  Diced red and yellow peppers
  Chopped tomatoes
  Diced red potatoes

Toss this mixture with a little olive oil, a generous sprinkling of basil, thyme, and oregano, a little salt and pepper, and a few dashes of balsamic vinegar (do not substitute another type of vinegar). Place each portion of fish and accompanying vegetables on a piece of parchment paper, large enough to overlap and twist closed. Make sure each one is tightly secured so that no liquid will escape. Bake for 10-12 minutes in a pre-heated 350 degree oven.

We have a friend from St. Lucia who loves to cook and can make up many a tasty meal in the galley of his sailboat. This is a particularly easy recipe that we inherited from him.

Karen Iaccarino

STEAMED SIZZLING FISH

1 lb. fish fillets (grouper or other firm fish)
6 Tbs. peanut oil
6 Tbs. soy sauce
Juice of half a lemon
1 clove garlic, minced
1 scallion, chopped fine

Steam fish until nearly done--do not overcook! Place steamed fish on a deep platter or casserole dish. Sprinkle minced garlic and chopped scallion over fish. Heat oil almost to smoking and pour over fish. Pour soy sauce mixed with lemon juice over fish.

This is also a great way to prepare vegetables such as broccoli, cauliflower, carrots, and green beans. The children will fight over the "pot likker."

Ted Rosengarten

The Red Boat, a painting by Aaron Baldwin.

During my boyhood years in McClellanville, I was not idle. I became a commercial fisherman, working alone. I learned the haunting names of the famous spots of the vast sea marsh, names such as Eagle Hummock, Oyster Bay, Five Fathoms Creek. On good days I might catch one hundred good fish that I could sell. I had my regular customers and sold a 'string' of twelve fish for twenty-five cents. I fished both by day and by night and loved the exhiliration and the adventure of it all. I remember how I loved to sell fish to a gentleman who weighed about three hundred pounds. He always bought a string for the family and one for himself.

Archibald Rutledge, *The Woods and Wild Things I Remember.*

CAPTAIN WILLIE'S
BARBECUED FISH

¾ cup mayonnaise
¼ cup mustard (Gray Poupon Spicy)
2 Tbs. horseradish
1 tsp. parsley
1 tsp. garlic powder
1 tsp. black pepper
Juice of half a lemon
Fish filets or fish steaks

Mix all together in a bowl and batter fish. The secret to cooking fish on the grill is to let your charcoal die down to a low heat. Place fish on the grill and cover with aluminum foil. This is very important because fish will dry out quickly. Let fish cook halfway through. Then uncover. Turn fish over with a spatula. Baste with batter and re-cover until done.

Willie Humphrey

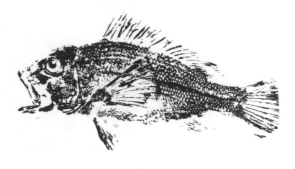

McClellanville is located on Jeremy Creek behind the marshes and islands that border the Atlantic Ocean. It's a beautiful village with its old, gray oaks and the sweet smell of seafood and salt water. You can go shrimping, casting, and fishing, or you can just sit on your porch, watching the creek and the ripples in it and enjoying the summer breezes.

From "The Village Guide: Places to Go, People to See," by the 6th grade of Archibald Rutledge Academy, 1988.

SEAFOOD SALAD

Use your favorite fish. You can use leftovers or boil fresh or frozen fish until it flakes. Drain and cool. If you crumble cooled fish you can usually remove all remaining bones. Add sweet relish, onion, celery, and your favorite mayonnaise and seasonings. Chill and serve. Tastes great on crackers or sandwiches.

Bernadette Humphrey

The making of salt was an ancient occupation on [Cape Romain]. The Seewee were reported trading salt in the 1500s, and it was their salt ponds at Awendaw that Governor Johnson had claimed in 1706, renaming the spot "Salthope." There was no record of his success or any indication that prior to the Civil War the manufacturing of salt was a profitable enterprise here. No doubt some local consumption was satisfied, but there was stiff competition. Ships sailing to England carried cotton and rice. Returning they brought manufactured goods, a small cargo which could be rounded out with a ballast of "good coarse salt." In Virginia there were salt "works" and in the Caribbean as well. . . . All along the shore that faced the Cape Marsh, slaves began boiling seawater in salt pots. The "pots" were actually steam boilers from the abandoned rice mills that had been cut in half and bricked about and given chimneys. Into these saltwater was placed and boiled day and night until salt was distilled. At first wooden boxes were used to hold water during low tide, but later salt ponds were dug where the water could be held to evaporate, thus concentrating its salt content.

William P. Baldwin, "Salt for the People"

MARINATED SHRIMP

Mix together and let marinate for at least 24 hours:
    3 lbs. cooked shrimp
    1 cup catsup
    1 cup vinegar
    ½ cup Wesson oil
    1 Tbs. sugar
    Salt and pepper to taste
    Several sliced carrot sticks
    1 Tbs. Worcestershire sauce
    Dash tabasco
    2 bell peppers in rings
    1 onion in rings
    1 tsp. celery seed
    2 bay leaves
    1 clove garlic, chopped
    2 Tbs. prepared mustard

When Allston and I were married, we started our own Christmas tradition that we hope to pass on to our children, Bochet and Eliza. Every year except 1989--when Allston's shrimp boat sat on the corner of Oak and Morrison streets-- Allston brings home fresh shrimp a couple of weeks before Christmas and we pickle shrimp to give to our family and friends. Bochet's favorite part is testing and decorating the pint mason jars we put them in.
Gerilyn Graham Leland

PICKLED SHRIMP AND ONIONS

5 lbs. fresh boiled shrimp
2 large red onions, sliced very thin
1 can pickling spice
White vinegar
Salt and sugar

Boil and peel shrimp. Using a fairly big container, put a layer of shrimp on the bottom. Layer some of the onion slices on shrimp. Keep layering shrimp, onions, and spices until full. Combine plenty of white vinegar with a cup or 2 of water. Add a little salt and sugar and pour over shrimp with vinegar solution. Let sit in fridge at least 4 hours (overnight is best). Serve with cream cheese and crackers.

Freddy Arthur

VEGETABLES

Richard T. Morrison, one of the few remaining full-time farmers in this area, has a beautiful field of beans beside the inland waterway near his home. Mexican bean beetles attacked the beans planted in the garden near the house, but this field, containing twenty-four acres, has been free of them. Over 3,300 crates of beans already have been picked, and were sold at the field. Beginning August 18, two varieties of seed were planted--black valentine and giant stringless. . . . The twenty acres planted in black valentines were affected by the dry weather and the first small beans dropped off, but the four and a half acres of giant stringless made steady progress. Picking began October 9, with seventy-five laborers in the field at a time, and continued through this week. . . . This field has had three crops this year. Seventeen acres were planted in Irish potatoes, and the remainder in tomatoes with lettuce between the rows. Laurel Hill, Mr. Morrison's home, is about five miles from McClellanville on the Charleston-Georgetown highway. It originally was an indigo plantation of 3,688 acres.

Article (probably from the Charleston *News and Courier*), reprinted in *The Visible Village*, by William P. Baldwin, 1984.

BUBBER'S BUTTER BEAN SOUP

1 lb. dried small butter beans or lima beans
Water
2 tsp. salt
Pepper to taste
2 tsp. ground ginger
Ham hock or meaty ham bone
4 Tbs. olive oil
1 onion, chopped
1 clove garlic, mashed
2 carrots, chopped
1 (10 oz.) pkg. frozen chopped spinach
1 cup diced potatoes
2 cups shredded cabbage

Soak beans in water overnight. Drain. Add enough water to cover plus about an inch over. Add the salt, pepper, ginger, and ham hock. Bring to a boil, then reduce to a simmer and cook 45 minutes. Remove the ham hock and cut off the meat. In a small saucepan heat the olive oil, add the meat from the hock, the onion, garlic, and carrots; sauté until tender, then add to the soup. Add the spinach, potatoes, and cabbage; simmer for 30 minutes or until vegetables are tender, adding a little water if need be. Correct seasoning and serve.
Adam Howard

OKRA SOUP

1 meaty beef bone
4 cups chopped okra
1 (28 oz.) can chopped tomatoes
1 chopped onion

Boil beef bone and onion in one quart water until beef is tender. Add okra and tomatoes. Salt and pepper to taste. Cook over low heat until okra is tender. Serve over rice.

Mary Scott

ARTICHOKE DIP

1 can artichoke hearts, chopped
1 cup mayonnaise
1 cup Parmesan cheese
1 tsp. garlic

Mix ingredients; bake at 350 degrees for 40 minutes. Put slivered almonds on top if desired.

Martha Zierden

QUICK MEXICAN DIP

8 oz. cream cheese, softened
1 (11½ oz.) jar Frito-Lay Chunky Medium
  Salsa

Have cream cheese at room temperature and
mash with a fork to soften. Blend in salsa,
continuing to stir until mixed with soft cheese.
Serve with crisp tortilla chips.

Cindy Buscemi

SPINACH DIP

2 cups mayonnaise
½ cup chopped green onion tops
½ cup parsley flakes
Squeeze of lemon
1 pkg. frozen chopped spinach
Salt and pepper to taste

Mix all ingredients and chill for several hours.
Make sure the water is squeezed out of the
frozen spinach.

Carolyn Page

ROSE WILLIAMS'
SWEET POTATO PONE

10 large whole sweet potatoes (grated, the old fashioned way) *or* 3 lbs. sweet potatoes, boiled and mashed
½ lb. butter or margarine
½ cup milk
½ lb. brown sugar
3 medium eggs
½ tsp. salt
1½ lbs. all-purpose flour
⅛ tsp. lemon juice (a dash)
⅛ tsp. nutmeg (a dash)
⅛ tsp. cinnamon (a dash)
1 cup molasses

Grate potatoes after washing. Mix everything together. Beat! Throw in a 20" x 20" pan. Bake at 350 degrees for about 30-40 minutes. To serve cut in squares. Serve cold.

Ruth Singleton Middleton

BOSTON BAKED BEANS

1 lb. dry kidney beans
1 cup molasses
½ cup dry mustard
1 ham hock or ham trimmings

Pick, wash, and soak beans overnight in 3 quarts of water. Add ham and cook in same water until tender, approximately 45 minutes. Add more water if necessary, just enough to cover. Add other ingredients. Pour into bean crock or baking dish and bake in 300 degree oven for at least 5 to 6 hours. The longer baked the better. Check several times to see if more water is needed. If so, add very little at a time-- usually ½ cup is sufficient. Delicious served with hamburgers, Boston brown bread, and a salad.

Bobbie Davis

GEORGIA-STYLE CABBAGE CASSEROLE

1 medium-size head of cabbage
1 large onion
1 cup cheese, grated
1 can mushroom soup

Steam cabbage and onion together, just until wilted. Salt to taste. Arrange a layer of cabbage mixture on bottom of casserole dish. Add layer of soup. Continue adding layers. Top with shredded cheese. Place in 350 degree oven until cheese is melted and casserole is bubbling hot, about 30 minutes.

Bobbie Davis

CHILIES RELLENOS

This is the classic way of preparing stuffed peppers, Mexican style. The peppers are Anaheim or poblano chilies, not bell peppers; they are stuffed with cheese, not with a rice-meat mixture, and they are coated in egg and deep fried instead of being baked in an oven. Four people can easily put away a dozen as a main course, and they are rather time-consuming to make if you use fresh chilies. On the other hand, canned chilies will not be anything like as good as fresh ones; use them only if you are desperate for time. Until you've had the real thing, you don't know what you're missing. You'll never order them in a restaurant again once you've made your own!

12 Anaheim or poblano chilies
1 lb. Monterey Jack cheese
1 cup all-purpose flour
6 eggs
Oil for frying

Roast and skin the chilies by placing them over an open flame, such as a barbecue. Otherwise, broil them in the oven--it works just as well. Keep turning the chilies as the skins blister and pop. Once the whole skin is blistered, place the chilies in a plastic bag, closing it tightly and allowing the chilies to steam for 15-20 minutes. Peel the skin from each chile. Then slit open the side of each and remove the seeds and veins. Be careful not to break the flesh. (I find it is easier to do this under running water, as the chilies are still quite hot at this point.) Into each chile insert a rectangular piece of cheese, tapering the end of the cheese slightly. Roll the peeled, de-seeded, stuffed chilies in flour. Beat the egg yolks and whites separately; the whites should be beaten to the stiff peak stage. Re-combine the eggs and beat together quickly. Dip the chilies in the egg batter, being sure to cover the whole surface evenly. Fry in hot oil that is more than 3" deep until browned on both sides. Drain on newspapers. Serve at once or keep warm in the oven until they are ready to serve.

Alison Reside

EASY EGGPLANT TART

1 eggplant
12 mushrooms
2 red onions
3 cloves garlic
3 scallions
Parsley
Cilantro
1 Tbs. fresh ginger root, minced
4 Tbs. olive oil
Salt and freshly ground black pepper
1 Boboli

Cut and sweat eggplant by salting it and allowing it to sit for a few minutes. Rinse and pat dry. Toss onions and garlic in olive oil until translucent; add minced ginger. Add eggplant and mushrooms and cook until tender but not soggy. Add salt and pepper. Cover Boboli with cooked mixture. Add parsley, cilantro, and scallions. Place under broiler until Boboli crust is warm, about 2-3 minutes.

Stephanie Waldron

EGGPLANT CASSEROLE

1 large eggplant
2 cups cracker crumbs
1 tsp. salt
1 (13 oz.) can evaporated milk
1 cup diced cheddar cheese
½ cup cooking oil
½ cup chopped onions
2 eggs
½ tsp. paprika
½ tsp. garlic

Pare and dice eggplant. Cover with water and boil until tender. Drain. Place in a large mixing bowl. Add soda crackers, salt, milk, cheese, oil, and onions. Mix lightly. Beat eggs and add to eggplant mixture. Pour into a 2-quart casserole and bake at 350 degrees for 45 minutes. If desired, sprinkle with garlic salt and paprika while still hot.

Sandy Reid Bigelow

STUFFED EGGPLANT

1 large eggplant (1½ lbs.)
¼ cup chopped onion
1 Tbs. butter or margarine
1 (10 oz.) can condensed cream of mushroom soup
1 Tbs. chopped parsley
½ Tbs. Worcestershire sauce
1 cup finely crushed rich round crackers (about 24)

Slice off one side of eggplant. Remove pulp to within ½" of the skin. Cook eggplant pulp in a *small* amount of boiling water 'til tender, about 10 minutes; drain thoroughly (even blot it). Cook onion in butter 'til tender but not brown. Add soup, eggplant pulp, parsley, Worcestershire sauce, and all of the cracker crumbs except 2 tablespoons. Fill eggplant shell with mixture. Place in baking dish (10" x 6" x 2"); sprinkle reserved crumbs over top. Carefully pour hot water in bottom of dish to depth of ½". Bake at 375 degrees 'til heated through, 50-60 minutes. Serves 4-6.

Ellen Baxter, from The Old Stone Inn, Simpsonville, Kentucky

SQUASH CASSEROLE

2 cups squash
¾ stick butter
2 eggs
½ cup chopped onion
1 cup grated cheese
¾ cup milk
Salt to taste
Pepper to taste
1½ cups crumbled Ritz crackers

Cook squash in salted water and mash before measuring. Mix with other ingredients. Top with a few more crumbled Ritz. Bake at 350 degrees for 40 minutes.

Nancy Morrison

GREEN PEA CASSEROLE

1 (17 oz.) can LeSeur peas, drained
1 can water chestnuts, chopped
1 small onion, chopped
1 can cream of mushroom soup
½ cup cheddar cheese, grated and divided
1 cup (½ stack) Ritz crackers, crushed
¾ cup butter or oleo, melted

Combine first 5 ingredients. Sprinkle some of the cheese on top. Sprinkle with crushed crackers and drizzle with melted butter. Bake at 400 degrees for 15 minutes. Serves 10.

Great ingredients to have on hand, especially when there are no decent fresh vegetables available.

Jackie Morrison, Laurel Hill Bed and Breakfast

ASPARAGUS SOUFFLÉ

1 can cut green asparagus, drained
1 can mushroom soup
1 scant cup mayonnaise
1 cup grated cheese
4 eggs

Blend all ingredients together in the blender. Pour into 1½-quart buttered casserole. Bake (uncovered) in a pan of hot water at 350 degrees for 1 hour.

Anne McQueen Mullikin

ZUCCHINI PIZZA

Slice zucchini squash lengthwise. Take a fork and poke holes all through the meat. Sprinkle soy sauce all over and then cover with Parmesan cheese. Bake at 350 degrees until tender. Really good!

Maggi Yergin

CHEESE BROCCOLI

2 pkgs. frozen chopped broccoli
2 beaten eggs
1 cup mayonnaise
½ cup milk
1 cup grated sharp cheddar cheese
1 can cream of celery soup
1 tsp. Accent
1 tsp. Worcestershire sauce
1 tsp. minced onion
Salt and pepper to taste
1 stack round buttery crackers, crumbled
Butter

Cook the broccoli according to package directions; drain. Combine remaining ingredients except cracker crumbs and butter. Mix with broccoli. Place in a greased casserole dish and sprinkle with crumbs. Dot with butter. Bake at 350 degrees for 45-50 minutes. Makes 10-12 servings.

Rossie Talley

BROCCOLI FONDUE

2 bunches green onions, chopped
2 sticks butter
2 cloves garlic, finely chopped
2 (8 oz.) cans mushroom pieces
2 pkgs. frozen broccoli flowerets
2 cans mushroom soup
2 rolls yellow garlic cheese
Salt and cayenne pepper to taste

Drain the mushrooms. Save the liquid. When the broccoli flowerettes have thawed, chop them. Add the mushroom liquid. Sauté the green onions and garlic in the butter. Add the mushrooms first, then mushroom soup. Add the broccoli flowerets, yellow garlic cheese, salt and pepper. Simmer the mixture until cheese melts. Serve with cubes of French bread. This recipe makes 2 quarts. It is easily cut in half.

Ellen Baxter

POTATO SALAD WITH CUMIN

1 lb. potatoes (about 3 large)
4 Tbs. peanut oil
½ tsp. cayenne pepper
½ tsp. salt
1 tsp. cumin
Pinch thyme
Juice of 1 lemon
1 clove garlic, minced

Boil the potatoes in their skins until tender. Cool and peel. Cut into ½" cubes. Heat the oil in a skillet; add the cayenne, salt, cumin, thyme, and garlic. Sauté gently and add the lemon juice. Bring mixture to a boil and pour over the potato cubes. Toss lightly. Refrigerate. Serve chilled or at room temperature. A traditional Sephardic dish from North Africa.

Ted Rosengarten

BROCCOLI SALAD

4 cups chopped raw broccoli
½ cup grated cheddar cheese
½ cup chopped onion (Vidalia is best)
8 strips fried bacon, crumbled

Dressing

1 cup mayonnaise
2 Tbs. vinegar
¼ cup sugar

Mix ingredients and chill. Allow to sit 2 hours before serving.

Martha Zierden

CHICK PEA SALAD

1 (16 oz.) can garbanzo beans, drained
4-6 oz. feta cheese, crumbled coarsely
1 small sweet onion, cut into half rings
2 medium ripe tomatoes, cut up
½ cucumber, sliced
½ cup calamata olives
Optional--capers, marinated mushrooms, artichoke hearts, or pickled hot peppers
½ cup Greek Dressing

Combine all ingredients except cheese and tomatoes in a bowl. When well mixed add tomatoes to the top and sprinkle the cheese on last. Leave the cheese and onions in large pieces, otherwise the small bits tend to sift to the bottom and get left. Dress with Greek Dressing. Serves 4-6.

Billy's Greek Dressing

½ cup balsamic vinegar
½ cup extra virgin olive oil (If olive oil is too strong for you, use other vegetable oil and add a teaspoon of olive oil for flavor.)
Juice of ½ lemon
Salt and pepper to taste
1 tsp. dried garlic or 3-4 cloves chopped fresh
1½ Tbs. oregano

Combine these at least 12 hours before serving.

Billy Dinwiddie

PASTA SALAD

Cook 1 lb. pasta shells or twists. Rinse under cold water until cooled. Add your favorite garden vegetables--I like to add whatever is in season, including squash, onions, peppers, peas, celery, and carrots. Pepperoni and shrimp make a tasty addition, as well as black olives, artichoke hearts, and garlic. Toss all ingredients and add Parmesan cheese, salt, and pepper to taste.

Dressing

¼ cup red wine vinegar
2 Tbs. water
¾ cup olive or safflower oil
Garlic
Fresh herbs from the garden

To vary this I sometimes use a ranch dressing or combine both dressings. I almost always add extra red wine vinegar--several healthy dashes.

The fun with pasta salad is the experimentation with what's in the garden or in season at the vegetable stand.

Bernadette Humphrey

TACO SALAD

1 #300 can Bush's Best Kidney Beans
1 lb. ground beef
¼ cup chopped onion
1 Tbs. chopped green chilies
8 oz. cheddar cheese, grated
1 bag taco chips, crumbled
2 tomatoes, diced
½ cup sliced ripe olives
1 head lettuce, torn into bite size pieces
1 (8 oz.) bottle Russian dressing

Cook ground beef until done, stirring to break into small pieces. Drain well on paper towels; salt and pepper lightly. Cool. Combine beef, drained beans, onion, chilies, tomatoes, and olives. Put lettuce in a large bowl and top with bean mixture. Sprinkle on cheese and taco chips. Pour dressing over. Toss well and serve.

Sherry Browne

"HOW TO WING" COLESLAW

No salt, no sugar, no vinegar.

Grate the following:
    1 head green cabbage
    ½ head red cabbage
    3 carrots
    1 large onion
    1 green pepper, finely chopped

Add mayonnaise, pepper, garlic powder, and sesame seed to taste. Add black or green olives as preferred.

Jeff Megginson

MARINATED SQUASH SALAD

5 medium squash, sliced thinly
½ cup onion, sliced (green onion if possible)
½ cup green pepper, sliced
½ cup celery, sliced

Combine the following, pour over the above, and chill at least 12 hours:
    ¾ cup sugar
    2 Tbs. red wine vinegar
    ⅔ cup cider vinegar
    1 clove garlic, crushed
    ⅓ cup oil
    ½ tsp. pepper
    1 tsp. salt

Great for summer picnics!

Jackie Morrison, Laurel Hill Bed and Breakfast

SEVEN-LAYER SALAD

Fry ahead 3 or 4 strips of bacon. Shred one head of lettuce and put in bottom of serving bowl. On top of the lettuce put the following in layers:

 ½ cup diced celery
 ½ cup chopped mild onion
 ½ cup chopped green pepper
 3 grated hard-boiled eggs
 1 (10 oz.) pkg. frozen peas, thawed and
  drained

Spread with 1 pint Miracle Whip salad dressing, then with 1 cup mayonnaise. Sprinkle with 2 Tbs. sugar and then with 6 oz. Parmesan cheese. Sprinkle grated egg and crumbled bacon on top. Cover tightly and refrigerate. You may add other layers if you like. I sometimes add a layer of black olives, cucumbers, and mushrooms, but try not to add too many as you want each serving to go from the top to the bottom and contain some of each layer.

Margaret Densmore

DELICIOUS DIFFERENT SALAD

8 cups salad greens (1 large head lettuce)
2 cups sliced oranges (2 large)
1 cup peanuts (Planters salted)
1 red onion in rings
3 medium bananas
1 green pepper

Dressing

Mix in blender:
   ¾ cup sugar
   1 tsp. salt
   1 tsp. dry mustard
   1 cup oil
   1 Tbs. celery seed
   ⅓ cup wine vinegar
   2 Tbs. lemon juice
   1 small chopped onion

Soak sliced bananas in orange juice and pat dry with paper towel so they won't turn dark. Add peanuts last. Toss with dressing just before serving.

Carrie Jean Price

Corn, a woodcut by Dale Rosengarten.

SALLY'S CORN SALAD

1 (12-oz.) can corn, drained
¼ cup chopped bell pepper
2 Tbs. diced pimiento
½ cup chopped celery
1 cup peeled, thinly sliced cucumber
½ cup thinly sliced Bermuda onion
⅓ cup vegetable oil
3 Tbs. sugar
1½ tsp. salt
3 Tbs. red wine vinegar

Combine first 6 ingredients. Combine remaining ingredients, stir well, and pour over vegetables. Toss, cover, and chill 8-10 hours. May be served in a bowl with a slotted spoon. I prefer to drain the mixture and serve on a bed of lettuce with fresh summer vegetables such as cherry tomatoes, radishes, and cold asparagus. Serves 4-6. I double this for a "village" Sunday dinner.

Sally Warren

On the weekend my grandfather worked in corn fields and grew corn and tomatoes.

Markel Woodfield, McClellanville Middle School

FROZEN CUCUMBER SLICES

3 cups sliced cucumbers
1 medium onion, sliced
2 Tbs. salt
1½ cups sugar
¾ cup white vinegar

Slice cucumbers and onions. Sprinkle them with salt. Mix well. Let stand in refrigerator 2 hours. Drain but don't rinse. About 1 hour before draining, mix sugar and vinegar. Heat until sugar dissolves. Cool. Pour over cucumbers and onions which have been put in freezer containers. Freeze. Thaw in refrigerator before using.

This is great in the winter after the summer's "cuke landslide."

Jackie Morrison, Laurel Hill Bed and Breakfast

My mother's first job in McClellanville was working in the bean field and cucumber field.

Telly Young
McClellanville Middle School

OKRA PICKLES

Okra, preferably all one size, about 4", cut leaving ¼" of stem on.

Place in the bottom of each pint jar:
  1 clove garlic or ¼ tsp. dried minced garlic
  1 tsp. dill seed
  1 hot pepper

Pack okra tightly in jars, stem end down.

Heat to boiling:
  1 quart white vinegar
  ½ cup salt
  1 quart water

Pour boiling mixture over okra. Leave ½" space at top and seal. Cook in boiling water bath about 10 to 15 minutes.

SQUASH PICKLE

8 cups small yellow squash, sliced
2 onions, sliced thin
4 bell peppers, diced
2 cups vinegar
3 cups sugar
2 tsp. mustard seed
2 tsp. celery seed

Mix squash, onions, and peppers well. Salt to taste. Let stand for 1 hour. Drain well. Bring to a boil the vinegar, sugar, mustard and celery seed. Pour over squash mixture. Bring back to a good boil. Remove from tin, place in hot sterile pint jars, and seal.

Minnie Cash

Sign for Preston Foxworth's vegetable stand, a photograph by Bernadette Humphrey.

DILLY BEANS

4 lbs. young tender beans
4 cups water
4 cups vinegar
8 large cloves garlic
8 hot pepper pods
8 large heads dill (or 1 tsp. dillweed per jar)
½ tsp. salt per pint jar

Steam beans. Wash and pack upright in sterilized jars. Add 1 clove of garlic, 1 pepper pod, 1 head of dill or dillweed to each jar (push down among beans), and ½ tsp. salt. Boil water and vinegar. Pour over beans. Seal at once. Process in boiling water bath for 5 minutes. Makes 8 pints.

Mertice Cumbee

MOM NAN'S CHOW CHOW

Grind:
    1½ pecks green tomatoes (4 lbs.)
    1 large head cabbage
    6 large red onions

Sprinkle through with ½ cup salt; let stand overnight. Drain and squeeze out all the water.

Grind and add:
    6 green peppers
    2 hot red peppers
    1 bunch celery
    ¼ cup mustard seed
    1 oz. celery seed
    ½ lb. brown sugar

Mix together and cover with vinegar. Fill clean, hot jars with mixture. If possible, put a small piece of horseradish root in each jar, or use ½ teaspoon prepared horseradish in top of each jar.

Jenna McClellan

York McGinnis pounds rice with a mortar and pestle, 1981, a photograph by Ted Rosengarten.

RICE
AND OTHER
GRAINS

The early decades of Afro-American basketry parallel the rise of rice cultivation on the southeastern coast. Even before Carolina was colonized, rice had been proposed as a staple for export. Around 1690, after two decades of experimentation, settlers began producing a "plausible yield," and by the mid-eighteenth century, rice was the principal crop of what was to become the wealthiest group of planters in America. From the start, lowcountry plantations proved to be friendly environments for the production of Afro-American sea grass baskets. Indeed, rice could not have been processed without a particular coiled basket, called the "fanner." The fanner was a wide winnowing tray used to "fan" rice--that is, to throw the threshed and pounded grain into the air or drop it from a basket held at a height into another basket, allowing the wind to blow away the chaff.

Dale Rosengarten, *Row Upon Row: Sea Grass Baskets of the South Carolina Low Country*, 1986

SHRIMP FRIED RICE

1 onion
Small bell pepper
2-3 cups cooked rice
Worcestershire sauce
Soy sauce
1 Tbs. butter
1½ lb. shrimp, peeled and deveined
Salt and pepper to taste

Sauté onion and bell pepper in butter until tender. Add shrimp and cook until slightly pink. Add a little Worcestershire sauce and soy sauce at a time, while crumbling rice into pan. There should be enough sauce to turn rice slightly brown. Salt and pepper to taste. I fix mine in an electric frying pan. It can be kept warm for a while if stirred.

Bonnie Morrison

CURRIED YELLOW RICE

1 cup rice
2 cups water (or part chicken stock and part
    water)
1 onion
1 tomato
1 bell pepper
2 Tbs. olive oil or other light oil
1 tsp. salt
1 tsp. good curry powder

Chop onion, tomato, and pepper. Put olive oil in a heavy pot, add onions, then turn on burner, and cook onions gently over medium heat until clear. Add tomato, pepper, salt, and curry powder. Stir this mixture to prevent sticking. Add rice and continue to stir for 4 or 5 minutes. Now add water, bring to a boil, cover, and let cook for 20 to 25 minutes as you usually do. A good side dish for fish or chicken. Cooking option--add 1½ cups peeled, washed shrimp during final 10 minutes of cooking to steam on top of rice for a one-pot meal.

Nancy Marshall McWilliams

CHILI PEPPER RICE CASSEROLE

1 (10 oz.) can chilies and tomatoes, drained
2 cups (1 large carton) sour cream
3 cups cooked rice
¾ lb. Jalapeño Jack cheese, cut in strips
½ cup grated cheddar cheese

Combine chilies, tomatoes, and sour cream. Alternate layers of rice, chili mixture, and Jack cheese. Top with cheddar and bake at 350 degrees for 25 minutes. Serves 8-10. I freeze leftover rice for casseroles. This is one of them!

Jackie Morrison, Laurel Hill Bed and Breakfast

Here [on the Santee] was built one of the first rice pounding mills of the world.
H.T. Morrison, quoted in *The Visible Village*

BROWN RICE

Put in casserole:
    1 cup rice (regular white)
    1 cup water
    1 can beef consommé
    1 tsp. salt
    1 small onion, chopped
    1 (4 oz.) can mushrooms (optional)
    ¾ stick oleo

Bake covered for 1 hour at 350 degrees or until moisture is absorbed.

Chip Hammans

My father grew rice in a low place, at the end of Old Collins Creek Road in South Santee. The soil was black and it was always damp. He was a carpenter--he used to build these trunks to let the water in and out. He used to make the mortar and the pestle that they beat the rice in.

Jane Wineglass

WILD RICE AND HAZELNUT SALAD

¾ cup wild rice
½ tsp. salt
½ cup hazelnuts (may substitute filberts)
5 Tbs. currants
Juice of 1 large orange
Citrus vinaigrette with hazelnut oil
1 small fennel bulb, cut into small squares
    (may substitute jicama)
1 crisp apple

Rinse wild rice, soak it for ½ hour, drain. Add salt and 4 cups water, bring to a boil. Simmer covered 30-35 minutes. Drain briefly in colander. Preheat oven to 350 degrees. While rice is cooking toast hazelnuts in oven 7-10 minutes, or until they smell toasty. Allow them to cool a few minutes, then rub with towel to remove most of the skins. Chop nuts into large pieces. Rinse currants in warm water, squeeze dry, then cover with orange juice and let them soak. Prepare vinaigrette (see recipe following). Add soaked currants and fennel to warm rice and toss with dressing. Just before serving, cut apple into small pieces, add it to the rice with hazelnuts, and toss. Season with fresh ground black pepper and salt if needed.

Citrus Vinaigrette
with Hazelnut Oil

Grated peel of 1 orange
4 Tbs. fresh orange juice
4 tsp. lemon juice
1 tsp. balsamic vinegar
½ tsp. salt
3 scallions (white parts only), minced
¼ tsp. fennel seeds, crushed under a spoon
5 Tbs. olive oil
1 Tbs. hazelnut oil
1 Tbs. chives, chopped
1 Tbs. chervil, chopped
1 Tbs. parsley, chopped

Put orange peel, orange juice, lemon juice, and vinegar in a bowl with salt, scallions, and crushed fennel seeds. Whisk in oils, then herbs. The dressing should be fresh and sparkly.

Stephanie Waldron

COLD RICE SALAD

4 cups chicken stock
2 cups uncooked rice
3 (6 oz.) jars of marinated artichokes
5 green onions
1 (4 oz.) jar pimento-stuffed green olives
1 large green pepper
3 stalks celery
¼ cup fresh parsely

Dressing

Artichoke marinade
1 tsp. curry powder
2 cups mayonnaise
Salt and pepper to taste

Cook rice in chicken stock. Cool. Chop and stir in other ingredients and dressing. Serve cold.

Martha Zierden

I went to Mt. Zion Church School in Santee. It was a vacant house. They told me to go on to the Mariner School. My parents sent me to night school. The fee was twenty-five cents a week. They paid for it with the bountiful harvest of rice--eight quarts.

Agnes Brown, age 105

LONG-BAKE RICE PUDDING

1 quart milk
¼ cup raw long-grain rice
½ cup white sugar
½ tsp. salt
½ cup raisins
1 tsp. vanilla
1¼ tsp. nutmeg

Combine the milk, rice, sugar, and salt in a buttered casserole. Bake uncovered for 2 hours, stirring every half hour. Add the raisins, vanilla, and nutmeg and mix gently. Bake for 30 minutes more, without stirring. Serve warm or cold.

Ted Rosengarten

BREAKFAST CASSEROLE

2 lb. bulk sausage (I use 1 hot and 1 regular Jimmy Dean)
1 cup raw grits, cooked
2 cups sharp cheddar cheese, grated
5 eggs
1½ cups milk
½ stick butter or margarine
Salt and pepper to taste

Brown and drain sausage and crumble in bottom of 9" x 13" greased casserole. Cook grits according to package directions (stiff is better than runny). Add oleo and cheese to cooked grits. Beat eggs, milk, salt, and pepper together and add to slightly cooled grits mixture. Pour over sausage in casserole. Bake at 350 degrees for 1 hour. I do this ahead and freeze it. I use the small Corningware "Grab-Its" and divide into 8 servings. Recipe can be halved. I make this for guests who swear they hate grits--they become converts to grits!

Jackie Morrison, Laurel Hill Bed and Breakfast

SEEWEE QUESADILLA

Soft tortilla
Grated Monterrey Jack cheese
Grated Mexican-style Velveeta cheese with
    jalapeños

Place mixture of cheeses on half of tortilla and flip other half over to make a half-moon shape. Fry 2 at a time in a hot pan with vegetable oil until tortilla is lightly browned and cheese is melted. Top with your choice of salsa and sour cream. For an added touch include some refried beans with your cheeses. Serve with chilled Corona and lime.

Kurt Penniger

CORNBREAD DRESSING

I usually make this in large quantities, so adjust as necessary to make a smaller amount.

1 large pan of cornbread, crumbled
6 slices of toast, finely ground
1 stalk of celery, chopped
2 cups onion, chopped fine
Parsley (for color)
2 sticks good margarine
12 hard-boiled eggs, chopped
Salt and pepper to taste
Poultry seasoning
Turkey broth to moisten and flavor

Have all ingredients at room temperature. Gently combine all ingredients except eggs and spices. Lift mixture with hands (do not pack). Add chopped boiled eggs. Add poultry seasoning, salt, and pepper. Bake on low heat until lightly browned. Serve with giblet gravy.

Irene Hathaway, Hathaway's Restaurant

BROCCOLI CORNBREAD

2 pkgs. Jiffy muffin mix
4 eggs
1 stick margarine
1 onion, chopped
10 oz. cottage cheese
1 tsp. salt
1 pkg. frozen broccoli, chopped

Boil broccoli 3 minutes, drain. Beat eggs, melt margarine, and mix all ingredients. Pour into a 13" x 9" baking dish and bake at 350 degrees for 40-50 minutes, until brown.

Anne McQueen Mullikin

MY FAVORITE BISCUITS

3 cups self-rising flour
2 tsp. baking powder
2 tsp. 10x sugar
½ cup vegetable shortening
1¼ cups buttermilk

Mix dry ingredients. Cut in shortening and stir in buttermilk. Knead a few times, then roll out on floured board or countertop. Cut into rounds; bake in preheated over at 450 degrees for 12 minutes. Brush with butter.

Nancy Morrison

CHEESE BEER BISCUITS

Bisquick
Beer
Sour cream
Cheese (medium cheddar)

Put Bisquick in bowl. Cup out a hole in the middle. Add shredded cheese. Add sour cream. Mix. Add beer. Combine with fork until barely incorporated. Bake at 350 degrees in preheated oven about 12-15 minutes until lightly browned.

Charlie Mauldin

BISCUITS SUPREME

2 cups all-purpose flour
4 tsp. baking powder
½ tsp. salt
½ tsp. cream of tartar
2 tsp. sugar
¾ cup shortening
¾ cup milk

Sift all dry ingredients together. Cut in shortening. Add milk all at once. Mix quickly. Let rest 2-3 minutes. (This is important.) Roll, cut, and place on ungreased baking sheet. Bake for 10-12 minutes in a 450 degree oven. Handle dough as little as possible.

Bobbie Davis

AWENDAW OR OWENDAW BREAD

This is my adaptation of an old plantation recipe. All the ingredients are still there--I only changed the measures and technique. It is not a thick cornbread--just an inch high or a little over--but it has a nice crust, top and bottom, and that wonderful spoonbread texture and taste inside. In other words, this "Awendaw" is a spoonbread you can slice, pick up with your fingers, even split and butter if you wish.

¼ cup grits, uncooked
1 cup water
3 Tbs. sweet butter
1 cup sweet milk
1 tsp. salt
1 cup enriched cornmeal
4 eggs, well beaten

In the top of a double boiler, pour in the grits and water; place over boiling water and cook until thick, stirring often. Add the butter to the grits, stirring until melted. Add the milk and salt. Stir and cook until the milk is hot; remove from the heat. Slowly add the cornmeal, beating well. The batter will be very thick and lumpy. Let the batter cool a little. With an electric mixer, beat in the eggs until fairly smooth. Pour into a well-buttered 9" cake pan and bake in a 350 degree oven for 45 minutes to an hour, until the top is deep golden brown. Slice into wedges and serve. Do not be alarmed if the bread begins to rise like a soufflé. It will not spill over the pan and will settle back down before the baking time is over. Serves 6 to 8.

Adam Howard

C DeAntonio

BOSTON BROWN BREAD

1 cup cornmeal
2 cups whole wheat flour
1 tsp. salt
¾ tsp. baking powder
2 cups buttermilk
¾ cup dark molasses
1 cup dark raisins

Butter well 2 (1 lb.) coffee cans. Combine flour, cornmeal, salt, and baking powder in a large bowl. Beat buttermilk and molasses until blended. Beat in flour gradually. Stir in raisins. Fill cans half full. Cover each with foil. Tie foil in place with string. Place cans in large kettle or pot; add water to reach halfway up the cans. Cover kettle. Steam over very low heat for 2½ hours, adding water as needed. Begin counting time after water has come to a boil.

Bobbie Davis

DELICIOUS OATMEAL BREAD

1½ cups boiling water
1 cup oats
¾ cup molasses
2 Tbs. butter
2 tsp. salt
1½ Tbs. yeast
2 cups warm water
1 or 2 cups whole wheat flour
6 or 7 cups unbleached flour

Boil oats in water for 20 minutes and let cool. Mix cooled oats with molasses, butter, salt, yeast, and 2 cups warm water. Sift in whole wheat flour. Rest for 30 minutes. Mix in remaining flour and knead for 15 minutes, adding flour as needed. Let rise for 30-40 minutes. Divide and make loaves. Let rise in pans for 20 minutes. Bake at 350-375 degrees for 35-40 minutes.

Susan Hindman

MISS EVE McCLELLAN'S
BREAD AND ROLL RECIPE

Dissolve 1 pkg. yeast in warm water with a pinch of sugar and set aside. Scald ½ cup of milk and add ½ cup of sugar and ½ Tbs. salt. Add 1 heaping Tbs. shortening or butter. Then add ½ cup cold water. Beat up 1 egg and gradually add warm milk solution to egg (so as not to curdle the egg). Add yeast to milk solution. Add all liquid to about 3 cups of *bread* flour. Add 1 cup--more or less--of flour until mixture can be turned out on counter and kneaded. Knead until elastic. The trick is not adding too much flour. Getting the feel of it takes time! Cover bowl of dough with plastic wrap and put in a warm place to rise (2 or 3 hours). Put dough into greased bread pan or roll out to about ½" thickness and cut into circles for rolls. Put rolls with sides touching on greased pan. Put in a warm place, covered with a dish towel, until well risen (1 or 2 hours). Brush tops with beaten egg yolk and a small amount of water. Bake at 300 degrees-- bread 50 minutes, rolls 20 minutes. Makes 1 loaf of bread or 12-16 rolls.

Alice DeAntonio

ITALIAN ROLLS

2 cups water
½ cup oil (not butter)
¼ cup sugar
1 Tbs. salt
⅓ cup warm water
2 cakes yeast
2 large eggs
6 cups flour

Heat 2 cups water to boiling. Pour over the oil, sugar, and salt. Cool until only lukewarm. Dissolve the yeast in ⅓ cup warm water. Add to cooled mixture along with the eggs and half the flour. Stir until smooth. Add the rest of the flour and blend in. Turn out onto a lightly floured breadboard and knead lightly. Shape into rolls and place them on buttered cookie sheets. Let rise until doubled. Bake in a 375 to 400 degree oven until golden brown--15 to 20 minutes. Note: If desired, brush with an egg white glaze and sprinkle with sesame or poppy seeds.

Lanie Youngman, from *A World of Breads* by Dolores Casella (New York: David White Co., 1966)

BANANA-ORANGE WHEAT BREAD

2 cups whole wheat flour
¼ cup wheat germ
1 tsp. salt
1 tsp. baking soda
3 large ripe bananas, mashed
½ cup orange marmalade (Smuckers low-sugar)
⅔ cup honey
⅓ cup Mazola oil
2 eggs, slightly beaten
1 tsp. vanilla extract
½ cup chopped pecans or walnuts

In large bowl, stir together flour, wheat germ, salt, and soda. In another bowl, mix bananas, marmalade, honey, oil, eggs, and vanilla. Stir liquid mixture into flour mixture, mixing only until dry ingredients are moistened. Add nuts.

Pour batter into greased 9" x 5" x 3" loaf pan. Bake in preheated 350 degree oven for 1 hour, or until done. Cool in pan 10 minutes; remove from pan and let cool completely on wire rack.

Cindy Buscemi

SWEET POTATO BREAD

2 cups sweet potato (boiled or baked, preferably baked)
2 cups regular flour (not self-rising)
1 tsp. baking powder
2 tsp. baking soda
1 tsp. salt
1 tsp. cinnamon
1 tsp. nutmeg
Pinch ginger
2 eggs
¾ cup sugar
¾ cup salad oil (preferably canola)
Chopped nuts (optional)

Sift flour with spices. Mix sugar, potato, and eggs. Beat until smooth. Add oil. Add flour and spice mixture. Fold in nuts if desired. Pour into greased bundt pan. Bake at 350 to 375 degrees for approximately 1 hour or until done.

I first created this when I was a single mother with four children in Los Angeles and my children wanted something sweet to eat.

Dorothy Talley

CINNAMON AND RAISIN
OR JELLY ROLL

2 cups warm milk
½ cup warm water
3 Tbs. yeast
1 cup sugar and honey
2 tsp. salt
2 Tbs. cinnamon
4 eggs
4 Tbs. oil
8 cups flour--plus

Warm milk. Dissolve yeast in water. Mix milk, sugar/honey, eggs, oil, and yeast mixture. Sift in 2 cups flour, cinnamon, and salt. Beat with egg beater. Rest 20 minutes. Sift in the rest of the flour slowly. Stir and knead until it's no longer sticky. Dough should feel alive! Divide and roll out. Fill with desired filling. Rise in pans for 30 minutes. Bake at 350 degrees for about 35 minutes. Rising time in winter is longer than in summer.

Susan Hindman

SOUTHERN PANCAKES

¾ cup flour
½ cup yellow cornmeal
1 Tbs. baking powder
2 Tbs. sugar
¾ tsp. salt
1 egg
1¼ cups milk
3 Tbs. melted shortening

Preheat heavy skillet or griddle on low temperature. Sift together dry ingredients in medium-size mixing bowl. In small bowl beat egg; add milk and shortening, mixing well. Slowly stir liquid into flour mixture, mixing only until dry ingredients are wet. Grease warm skillet lightly. Ladle or pour batter into small piles. Cook on low heat until tops are bubbly and bottoms are lightly browned. Turn and brown lightly.

Cindy Buscemi

Hogkilling, 1987, a photograph by Ted Rosengarten.

MEAT, POULTRY, AND GAME

Let me tell you of the "lunch rooms" and the "school lunches" in those days gone by. Each child came to school with his pockets bulging with sweet potatoes. Those children from across the swamp set traps along their route and came with half a dozen or more swamp "sporrows," as they called them. The "sporrows" were neatly dressed and hung on strings before the open fireplace. The potatoes were wrapped up in the ashes. By lunchtime, the children had a feast of steaming hot potatoes and nicely roasted birds.

H.T. Morrison in the Charleston *News and Courier,* quoted in *The Visible Village.*

ITALIAN PORK ROAST

4 lbs. pork roast (or roasting hen)
6 cloves garlic, sliced
4 sprigs rosemary
½ cup red wine vinegar
1 heaping Tbs. peppercorns
3 Tbs. olive oil
Salt to taste

Brown roast in olive oil in a heavy lidded pot. Add remaining ingredients. Simmer 2 hours, adding a little water as needed and turning frequently. Slice meat. Strain and de-grease drippings and pour over meat.

Sara Graham

SAL'S PORK STEW

4 (14½ oz.) cans pasta-style stewed tomatoes
   (Del Monte)
1 Tbs. Greek seasoning
1 tsp. garlic powder
2 lbs. lean pork (or pork chops)
4 large bell peppers, cut in ½" strips
3 large onions, cut in ½" strips

Place tomatoes, Greek seasoning, and garlic powder in stock pot on low heat; simmer slowly. Remove any bones, trim away fat, and cut pork into 1-inch strips or chunks. Brown in skillet using small amount of oil. Remove browned pork from skillet using slotted spoon and add it to tomatoes in stock pot. Add bell pepper strips to same skillet in which pork was browned; sauté lightly, retaining crispness. Add onion strips to skillet; sauté lightly. Using slotted spoon to drain off oil, remove pepper and onion slices from skillet and add them to the tomato mixture in the stock pot. Cover pot and simmer slowly over low heat for approximately 2½ hours. Serve over rice.

Sal Buscemi

BAKED PORK CHOPS

6 pork chops, cut 1" thick
1 bottle Russian salad dressing
1 pkg. dried onion dressing
1 small jar apricot preserves

Wipe pork chops with damp cloth. Place on baking dish. Mix Russian dressing, dried onion mix, and apricot preserves. Pour over pork chops. Bake for 1 hour in 350 degree oven, uncovered.

Dot Porter

October 13, 1918--Dear Pa, . . . I may farm with you when this war is over and things look very bright for an early ending. . . . We could make a good living when things are fixed up there as a start, two good mules (no dead horses), fifteen head of cattle, twenty-five head of sheep, ten head of hogs including a few sows, one Ford Auto. This will give us a good start to do real business. Some dream.

Tom Seabrook to his father, quoted in *The Visible Village*

ITALIAN SAUSAGE

3 lbs. boneless Boston butt, ground
½ oz. fennel seed
¾ oz. dried minced garlic
1 tsp. salt
7-10 red chili peppers, diced with seeds

Mix thoroughly and roll into sausages by hand (1¼" by 5"). Makes 16 sausages. Use immediately or wrap individually in wax paper and put in square quart containers for freezing.

Billy Dinwiddie

On a hog you eat everything but the squeal.

Ila Mae Cumbee

DEEP DISH PIZZA

1 lb. bulk pork sausage
1 can crescent rolls
1½ cups mozzarella cheese
1 (4 oz.) can mushrooms, drained
¼ cup green pepper, chopped
¼ cup catsup
¼ tsp. basil
¼ tsp. oregano
¼ tsp. fennel seeds (optional)
Sprinkle of Parmesan cheese

Brown sausage and drain. Press dough in ungreased 9" pie pan. To sausage add 1 cup mozzarella cheese, mushrooms, green pepper, catsup, and herbs. Spoon into crust. Top with ½ cup mozzarella and sprinkle with Parmesan. Bake at 325 degrees for 30-35 minutes. Let stand 5 minutes before cutting. Serves 6. Easy and great with a tossed salad!

Jackie Morrison, Laurel Hill Bed and Breakfast

THE "ANYONE-CAN-DO-IT IN-TWO-MINUTES-FLAT" QUICHE LORRAINE

1 frozen 9" unbaked pie shell
4 eggs, slightly beaten
1 cup cream or half-and-half
½ tsp. salt
⅛ tsp. cayenne
6 slices bacon, cooked crisp and crumbled
½ cup cheese, shredded

Combine filling ingredients and mix well. Place pie shell on a cookie sheet and set on rack in oven. Pour in mixture. Bake at 350 degrees for 30 to 35 minutes or until a knife inserted halfway between center and outside edge comes out clean. Makes 4 main dish servings, or 8 appetizer wedges, or *hors d'oeuvres.*

Bobbie Davis

HARVEST STEW

2 lbs. boneless beef cut into 1" cubes
¼ cup all-purpose flour
1½ tsp. salt
⅛ tsp. pepper
⅛ tsp. ground cloves
3 Tbs. vegetable oil
3 medium tomatoes, peeled and quartered
    or 1 (16 oz.) can whole tomatoes
1 cup beef broth
1 small pumpkin, about 10" in diameter
4 medium potatoes, peeled and quartered
8 small white onions, peeled
1½ to 2 cups green beans

Shake meat in a bag with flour, salt, pepper, and cloves. Heat oil in a heavy sauce pan; add meat and brown on all sides over high heat. Add tomatoes and broth. Simmer, covered, about 1½ hours or until meat is almost tender. Cut off pumpkin top and reserve. Remove seeds and membrane--scoop out pumpkin meat in chunks to measure 2 cups, being careful to leave pumpkin walls about ½" thick, especially near the bottom, so that pumpkin shell will not collapse during cooking. Stir pumpkin chunks, potatoes, onions, and beans into beef mixture. Bring to a boil. It's best to cook this on top of the stove until almost tender and then in the pumpkin for allotted time. Spoon stew into pumpkin shell and cover with reserved pumpkin top. Place pumpkin shell into a baking pan and bake in 350 degree preheated oven for about 45 minutes or until meat and vegetables are tender. Garnish with toasted pumpkin seeds.

Toasted Pumpkin Seeds

Seeds of 1 pumpkin
2 Tbs. vegetable oil
Salt to taste

Rinse seeds to remove strings and pulp; pat dry with paper towels. Spread on baking sheet and let dry for several hours. Preheat oven to 350 degrees. Toss seeds with oil and salt; toast in warm oven, stirring every 5 minutes until golden brown (about 25 minutes). Let cool completely. Taste and add salt if needed. Use to garnish or as a snack.

Ellen Saum, Jeremy Creek Café

BOBBIE'S HAM DELIGHTS

½ lb. butter, softened
3 Tbs. poppy seed
1 tsp. Worcestershire sauce
3 Tbs. prepared mustard
1 medium onion, grated
1 lb. ham, thinly sliced
3 pkgs. Pepperidge Farm party rolls

Mix butter, poppy seeds, prepared mustard, onions, and sauce. Split rolls and spread with preceding mixture. Fill with ham. Heat in oven at 300 degrees before serving.

Helpful hint: Cut ham in slices, 3 lengthwise and 4 slices across, before separating. Slice rolls before separating and they will be easier to handle. Five packages of rolls takes 2 (10 oz.) packages of ham. Eight packages of rolls takes 1 lb. of butter and 3 (10 oz.) packages of ham. There are 20 rolls to a package. May be prepared days in advance and refrigerated until needed.

Bobbie Davis

WHITLOCKS' SPECIAL STEAK AND SAUCE

1 2" sirloin steak
1 stick margarine
3 Tbs. garlic salt
1 large bottle A-1 sauce
1 large bottle Worcestershire sauce
½ cup water
½ cup vinegar
2 Tbs. black pepper

Melt margarine and garlic salt in saucepan. Heat until bubbly. Add A-1 sauce, Worcestershire sauce, water (I rinse sauce bottles with water), and vinegar. Sprinkle pepper on top of sauce. Bring to a boil. Set aside and cool. Pour cooled sauce over steak and marinate at room temperature for 12-24 hours. Cook steak on grill to preferred doneness, basting generously with sauce while cooking. Remaining sauce may be frozen and used again. It's excellent on grilled hamburgers.

Minnie Cash

COUNTRY-STYLE STEAK CASSEROLE

6 pieces cubed round steak (about 1 lb.)
1 can cream of mushroom soup
1 large onion, sliced
1 small can sliced mushrooms, drained, if desired

Coat beef with flour seasoned with salt and pepper. Brown beef in oil. Remove from drippings and place in a baking dish. Top each piece of beef with a slice of onion. Add soup and ½ can water to hot drippings to make gravy. Stir until mixed well and gravy thickens. Add mushrooms. Pour over steak, cover and cook 1 hour at 350 degrees. Serve over hot rice. Very hearty dish--favorite of men and growing boys.

Jo Luquire

BEEF STROGANOFF

¾ to 1 lb. boneless sirloin steak
1 onion, thinly sliced
2 Tbs. butter or margarine
1 (4 oz.) can sliced mushrooms
¾ cup water
1 cup brown gravy mix
1 tsp. paprika
½ cup dairy sour cream

Cut beef into thin strips. Cook beef and onions in butter until meat is slightly browned. Stir in water, mushrooms (including liquid), gravy mix, and paprika. Simmer for 5 minutes, stirring occasionally. Add sour cream; heat, but do not boil. Serve over rice or noodles. 4-5 servings.

Mertice Cumbee

CHICKEN-SAUSAGE PILAU

4 large chicken breasts, split
2 cups raw long-grain rice
1 small onion, sliced
3 tomatoes, peeled and diced
½ bay leaf
1 tsp. sweet basil
½ carrot, sliced
Salt and pepper
½ tsp. dried marjoram
½ lb. smoked sausage, cooked and sliced
4 Tbs. butter
1 cup chopped celery
4 cups rich chicken broth
1 large onion, chopped
1 green pepper, chopped

Cover chicken with 4 cups water; add small onion, bay leaf, carrot, and marjoram and simmer covered until chicken is tender. Strain broth and reserve. Skin, bone, and cut up chicken meat. Melt butter in a skillet over medium heat; add celery, onion, and green pepper. Cook 1 minute, stirring. Add rice, stirring constantly to prevent burning, until vegetables are tender. Turn off heat, stir in tomatoes and herbs, and season to taste. Pour into a large casserole; top with sausage. Arrange chicken on top. Add reserved chicken broth or a little more to make 4 cups. Cover and bake in a 350 degree oven 25 minutes, or until rice is tender and all liquid absorbed. Lightly stir with a fork to release steam before serving. Serves 8. I dare you to throw a handful of shrimp into this, too!

Adam Howard

CHICKEN CASSEROLE

1 stick margarine
1 pkg. Pepperidge Farm stuffing
1 can cream of mushroom soup
1 can cream of chicken soup
2 cups chicken broth
4 large chicken breasts, cooked

In a large baking dish, melt margarine, then sprinkle half of stuffing on bottom. Add mushroom soup and 1 cup of broth. Spread over it the chicken that has been cooked, cut up, and boned. Pour chicken soup and remaining broth over chicken. Sprinkle remaining stuffing over top and bake at 350 degrees for 45 minutes.

Rosemary Fitze

CHICKEN AND VEGETABLES

1 large broiler/fryer
1 large onion, cut in small wedges
4 small white potatoes, peeled and quartered
¼ cup self-rising flour (scant)
1 cup water
Salt and pepper to taste
About ½ stick of butter or margarine

Split chicken down the back; wash and season. Place in baking pan. Sprinkle flour over the chicken and dot with butter. Place the potatoes and onions around the chicken, season, and put water into the pan. Cover the pan and bake at 375 degrees until done, about an hour. Uncover pan for last few minutes to brown. This makes a good dish with gravy to eat on rice.

A recipe of Mrs. T.W. Graham, Sr., submitted by Kathy Graham Leland

CHICKEN DIVAN

1 whole chicken
2 pkgs. frozen broccoli spears
1 cup mayonnaise
1 cup cream of mushroom soup
1 cup cream of chicken soup
½ cup cheddar cheese, shredded
½ cup soft bread crumbs
1 Tbs. lemon juice
½ tsp. curry powder

Stew chicken until tender. Let cool. Cook broccoli as directed on package. Combine soups, mayonnaise, lemon juice, and curry powder. Place boned, cut-up chicken on top of broccoli in a casserole dish. Spread soup mixture over this. Add shredded cheese, then breadcrumbs. Bake uncovered for 30 minutes at 350 degrees.

Margaret Leland

CHICKEN MADALYN

1 good-size chicken, boiled in water with:
    1 cut-up onion
    Salt and pepper
    Lots of garlic salt
    ½ tsp. curry powder

Pick meat off bones into bite-size pieces. Save broth. Cook 2 (6 oz.) packages Uncle Ben's long-grain and wild rice with:
    2 cups chicken broth
    1 cup white wine
    1¼ cups water

Combine chicken pieces and rice with:
    1 can cream of mushroom or chicken soup
    8 oz. drained canned mushrooms
    8 oz. sour cream

Warm on top of stove and eat. Great left over. Makes lots.

Chip Hammans

MULLIGATAWNY (PEPPER WATER)

This India-born creation came to us via the sailing ships and was the rage a century ago.

2 Tbs. butter
½ cup onion, finely chopped
¼ cup green pepper, finely chopped
1 small clove of garlic, cut in half
2 Tbs. flour
1 Tbs. curry powder
1 pint half-and-half
1 qt. chicken broth
1 Granny Smith apple, peeled and chopped
1 Tbs. salt
Black pepper to taste

In the pot the soup will be cooked in, melt the butter, add the onion, green pepper and garlic, and cook over low heat until they are soft, but not brown. Remove the garlic, add the flour and curry powder, and cook 2 minutes, stirring. Add the milk, chicken broth, and apple. Blend well. Cook over hot water until smooth. Now if you want to make this "good enough to make you bite your Grand-maw," add a little diced, cooked, left over chicken. Serves 6.

Adam Howard

BAKED CHICKEN BREASTS

2 pkgs. boned chicken breasts
1 can cream of chicken soup
½ can evaporated milk
Swiss cheese
Pepperidge Farm Herb Dressing
½ stick margarine

Place cheese on top of chicken breasts. Mix chicken soup and milk. Pour over breasts. Top with herb dressing and melted margarine. Bake covered at 350 degrees for 1½ hours. May add pimento or red bell pepper for color.

Betty Bonner

FRIED CHICKEN

Clean chicken pieces thoroughly (no hair, no junk). Wash several times. Sprinkle salt, pepper, and Accent (optional). Beat 2 eggs in 2 cups of milk. Pour over chicken. Add flour. Coat real good. Put in dry flour. Cook in fryer for 15 minutes at 300 degrees. 12 servings.

Irene Hathaway, Hathaway's Restaurant

ROASTED ROSEMARY CHICKEN

1 broiler, whole
Sprigs of fresh rosemary
Salt
Pepper
Olive oil

Preheat oven to 400 degrees. Rinse and pat dry chicken. Save giblets for gravy stock if desired. Put broiler breast-side up in roasting pan or lightly oiled iron skillet. Rub over with olive oil. Lift up skin here and there and place rosemary under skin in as many places as possible. Sprinkle liberally with salt and pepper and any remaining rosemary. Roast one hour. Skin will be crispy and fragrant with rosemary. Serve with rice or a good bread to "sop up" the juices.

Nancy Marshall McWilliams

POPPY SEED CHICKEN

2 lbs. chicken, cooked and boned
8 oz. sour cream
1 can chicken soup
1½ cups Ritz crackers, crushed
1 Tbs. poppy seeds
1 stick oleo

Place cut-up chicken in casserole. Mix sour cream and chicken soup and pour over chicken. Mix cracker crumbs, poppy seed, and melted oleo; sprinkle over top. Bake at 350 degrees for 30-35 minutes.

Rossie Talley

ANNA'S CHICKEN PIE

This is an old recipe which was taught to Anna Geathers at the age of 13 by Mrs. "Pet" McClellan about 90 years ago. Anna made many superb dishes but could not tell how they were prepared. To learn we had to watch her.

4-5 lb. baking hen
1 average onion
1 Tbs. diced bell pepper
Salt and pepper
Prepared pastry (1 pie crust shell)
2 hard-boiled eggs

Cut chicken into sections and with onion, salt and pepper, and enough water to cover, cook in covered saucepan. Let simmer until chicken can be removed from the bone. Line deep baking dish with thin pastry. Place a layer of meat, several slices of boiled egg, and a few pieces of bell pepper alternately with a layer of thin pastry strips, until bowl is filled to within an inch of the top, ending with pastry. Cover pie with seasoned stock. Bake at 300 to 350 degrees until golden brown. For best results there must be a good supply of stock. Hot stock may be added while pie cooks. Pastry should be thin not to absorb all the stock.
Harriette Leland

GLAZED SKILLET CHICKEN

This is an easy and fast way to cook chicken and one of our favorite recipes.

1 (3 lb.) broiler-fryer chicken, cut into pieces
Salt and pepper
¼ cup salad oil
¼ cup mild-flavored honey
¼ cup freshly squeezed lemon juice
¼ tsp. paprika
½ tsp. dry mustard

Wipe chicken pieces well with damp paper towels. Season with salt and pepper. Brown chicken on both sides in heated oil in 10" skillet. Cover and cook over medium heat for 15 minutes. Combine remaining ingredients and pour over chicken, turning to coat. Continue cooking uncovered about 20 minutes. Baste frequently with sauce to glaze chicken. 4 servings.

Mertice Cumbee

NANA'S PATÉ

This recipe was given to me several years ago by Nana Reid and has become a great hit. I'm asked to bring it to every party or reception to which I'm invited. This paté goes a long way and fortunately it freezes well. I try to keep some on hand--you never know when the next party will be.

1 lb. bacon
6-8 cloves garlic
3 Tbs. dried basil
2 rolls of Braunschwager sausage
3 to 4 Tbs. Grand Marnier or brandy
2 lbs. chicken livers
2 medium onions
Salt and pepper
1 stick butter (not margarine)

For garnish:
    Lettuce leaves
    Black olives
    1 dozen eggs, hard-boiled
    Cherry tomatoes
    Bell pepper

It is best to start the paté a full day or two before the party. It gives the flavors more time to meld. Fry bacon until crisp. Remove and reserve bacon; pour off all but 2 tablespoons of bacon drippings. Melt butter in fat. Sauté diced onions and garlic in bacon drippings until translucent. Stir in basil and salt and pepper to taste. Add chicken liver mixture and sauté until done. Do not cook until hard. Cool liver mixture and refrigerate several hours or overnight. The next day chop reserved bacon finely in food processor, then add the liver mixture and the Braunschwager sausage; process until well mixed. Add the brandy or Grand Marnier to taste. Divide the paté into serving portions approximately the size of a small grapefruit. It is best to mold the portions in a bowl lined with plastic wrap, and refrigerate until set, approximately 3 or 4 hours or overnight. At this point you may freeze any portions if they are securely wrapped in plastic wrap. Use frozen portions within 3 or 4 months. Unmold paté onto lettuce-lined plates. Leave enough room on the plate to surround the paté with crackers. Wheatsworth are best. Chop boiled eggs (4 or 5 for each paté portion) and mold to outside of paté. Create flowers from cherry tomatoes and black olives, and leaves from bell pepper, to garnish.

Sara Lewis-Harken

June 16, 1863--Dear Wife, We have been faring sumptuously for a few days, having plenty to eat except bread. Our meal was so musty we could not make use of it, though we have rice a plenty. We have had bacon, potatoes, beans, squash, beef a plenty, and a few messes of venison. The boys kill a deer every week to two. We are getting pretty tired of beef. I think if I was at home and had such beef as we get here fried, well, I would then like it.

James Michael Barr to his wife from an encampment in McClellanville, *A Confederate Correspondence,* edited by Ruth Barr McDaniel.

Lee Arthur

MOSS SWAMP <u>HOT</u> VENISON SAUSAGE

3 lbs. ground venison
1½ lbs. fresh pork sausage
½ large onion, chopped
2 Tbs. red cayenne pepper, chopped
½ oz. apple cider vinegar
2 tsp. salt or salt substitute

Mix ingredients by hand thoroughly. Make into patties and freeze in quart ziplock bags, 4 to each bag. Makes 24 to 30 sausage patties.

Dan Wheeler

Out here if a man is able to go into the woods and creeks, the only things he has to buy are grits and rice.

Charles Williams, Awendaw

MOSS SWAMP VENISON STEW

5 lbs. venison
2 lbs. onions, chopped
2 large bell peppers, chopped
5 lbs. cut-up potatoes with peelings left on
Salt and pepper as desired

Boil meat from bones in 1 gallon of water; remove bones and add onions, 'taters, bell peppers, salt, and pepper. Cook on low heat, stirring frequently until stew becomes thoroughly mixed and thick. Serves 4 to 8. For added Low Country flair mix in 2 lbs. of chopped boiled shrimp when the stew is almost done.

Dan Wheeler

Come to McClellanville, the Historic Town. In Summer, Sea Breeze, Bathing, and Fishing; in Winter, Duck, Turkey, and Deer Shooting.

From an early Town of McClellanville letterhead, reproduced in *The Visible Village*

MOSS SWAMP
SQUIRREL OR RABBIT PILOU

4 cleaned squirrels or 2 small cleaned rabbits
   (2-3 lbs.)
2 large onions, chopped
Salt and pepper
4 cups rice

Boil meat and onions in a large pot until meat falls off the bones. Remove meat and store. Remove bones. Strain and save ingredients and save the water (6 cups). Cook rice in saved water, then add cooked meat, onions, salt and pepper, and just a good touch of Louisiana hot sauce. Feeds 6 well if ya hungry!

Dan Wheeler

SMOTHERED RABBIT

Cut up rabbit. Roll pieces in flour and brown in fat. Cover with water and simmer until meat is tender. The leavings in the pan will make for a good milk gravy for biscuits.

Maggi Yergin

PAN FRIED RATTLESNAKE

Thaw rattlesnake, minus head. Cut into small pieces. Dip snake in egg wash mixture (1 egg, ½ cup milk). Dredge each piece of snake through crumb mixture of your choice. I prefer to use regular breadcrumbs. Place snake in preheated pan which contains a good bottom covering of butter. It's important to use butter instead of oil or margarine for nice even browning. Turn snake to brown evenly on both sides. I like to eat it by itself, but you can serve it up with tartar sauce or any other condiments.

Jane Wineglass

Wild hogs and cattle, rice birds, possum, coon or fox, anything that moved was considered game, but it was turkey hunting that came under the heading of art. Shot from trees in the moonlight, called up to a blind with a hollow reed, a leaf or a cedar turkey box, matching wits with a wily gobbler was perhaps the truest test of a man.

William P. Baldwin, *The Visible Village*

ROAST RACCOON

Skin and clean raccoon. Remove parts not needed. Boil with salt and pepper and 1 tsp. vinegar in a deep pot for about 1 hour, depending on size. Roast in oven at 350 degrees for about 1 hour or until done. (Test for brownness and tenderness.) Baste occasionally. Roast covered until last 15 minutes for brownness. Season as you wish. I've used white potatoes or sweet potatoes, a dash of pepper, a dash of salt, a small or medium bell pepper, 2 large onions, 2 celery stalks, and 1 small clove garlic. Be sure to use juice from boiling to make a gravy by adding 1 cup of flour. Cut up and serve.

This is the way my grandmother taught me, Rose Williams, 1896-1984.

Ruth Singleton Middleton

'GATOR

The hardest part about cooking alligator is finding a cooperative one. Once you have succeeded in doing that, you'll find that most of the meat is in the tail. Actually the whole 'gator can be eaten if it's big enough.

Skin the tail. The meat is a fibrous white tissue. We usually slice it real thin, flip in flour, and fry. 'Gator tends to be rather tough so some folks like to soak it overnight in vinegar and water. I'd rather beat it with a meat mallet. (It's quicker and also helps relieve tension).

Maggi Yergin

Lee Arthur

SUGAR, FRUIT, AND NUTS

This is the time when pecans
Begin to fall.
One by one at first
They strike my tin roof
And roll down.

Then in early or mid-November
A strong gust whips up
Tearing at limbs and Spanish moss
And pecans rain down like hail.

Now it's pecan gathering time.
No more casually picking one up
As we pass by on some errand.

Chill evenings and warm kitchens,
And the smells of pecan-filled
Fudge and brownies,
And pecans salted and toasted brown.

J.O. McClellan III, from "Pecan Gathering Time"

BLACK WALNUT PIE

3 eggs
⅔ cup sugar
Dash of salt
1 cup dark corn syrup
⅓ cup butter or margarine
1 cup black walnuts

Beat eggs thoroughly with sugar, salt, syrup, and melted butter. Add black walnuts. Pour into unbaked pie shell. Bake in a 350 degree oven for 50 minutes or until knife inserted comes out clean. Cool.

Dot Porter

MAMA'S KARO NUT PIE

1⅓ cups pecans, large pieces
1 unbaked pie shell
¼ stick butter (not margarine)
1 cup sugar
3 eggs, slightly beaten
⅔ cup white Karo
⅓ cup Mrs. Butterworth's syrup
Pinch salt
1 tsp. vinegar, optional (to cut sweetness)
1 tsp. vanilla

Break up pecans and spread over an unbaked pie shell. Cream butter and sugar. Add eggs and beat well. Mix remaining ingredients and pour over pecans. Bake at 425 degrees for 10 minutes. Lower tempera ture to 350 degrees and cook approximately 1 hour, maybe less. If a knife comes out clean, it's ready.

Chip Hammans

DUTCH APPLE PIE

1 stick butter
1 cup sugar
2 Tbs. flour
1 tsp. cinnamon
5 or 6 sliced apples
1 egg white

Cream butter and sugar. Add flour and cinnamon. Spread half on bottom of unbaked crust. Slice apples thin and pile high over this. To other half of sugar mixture add 1 egg white, beaten stiff. Spread over top of apples. Put lattice or solid pie crust over top. Bake at 350 degrees for 30 to 40 minutes. May be served with ice cream or slices of cheese.

Some fifty years ago, this pie was a speciality at a restaurant in my home town of Meridian, Mississippi.

Dot Best

DIABETIC APPLE PIE

5 or 6 apples
2 Tbs. frozen apple juice
1½ Tbs. Equal
1 Tbs. flour
1 tsp. cinnamon or spice to taste
1 Tbs. butter
½ tsp. lemon juice
1 recipe for 2-crust pastry

Mix all ingredients. Pour into pastry-lined pan. Cover with remaining pastry. Bake at 450 degrees for 10 minutes, then at 400 degrees for 25 minutes or until juice bubbles through steam holes.

Mertice Cumbee

HAWAIIAN DREAM PIE

2 baked pie shells
1 (no. 2) can crushed pineapple
6 level Tbs. flour
1 cup sugar
3 bananas
1 cup chopped pecans
1 (3½ oz.) can Angel Flake coconut
1 Tbs. lemon juice
Pinch salt
Cool Whip or whipped cream

Mix flour and sugar together thoroughly. Add pineapple and juice and cook until thick. Let cool. Add salt. Slice bananas in pie shells, sprinkle with lemon juice, cover this layer with pecans, then spread the pineapple mixture over pecans. Next cover the layers with coconut; spread with Cool Whip. Refrigerate overnight.

Jo Luquire

MOCK COCONUT PIE

1½ cups milk
4 eggs
2 tsp. coconut extract
1 cup sugar
½ tsp. lemon extract
½ tsp. salt
1 cup spaghetti squash, cooked and separated
 into strands with fork
2 (9") pie crusts

Beat eggs well. Add milk, extracts, sugar, and salt. Mix well, then add squash, making sure it is stirred well into custard. Pour into pie shells. Bake at 350 degrees 45 minutes or until well browned. Makes 2 (9") pies.

Robyn Dudley

LEMON MERINGUE PIE

6 eggs
2½ cups sugar
1 cup cornstarch
1 tsp. salt
4 cups boiling water
⅔ cup lemon juice
1 tsp. butter
12 Tbs. sugar

Separate eggs. Save whites. Beat yolks. Mix sugar, cornstarch, and salt; gradually add boiling water. Cook over medium heat until mixture has the consistency of paste, about 10 minutes. Stir constantly. Add beaten yolks, lemon juice, and 1 tsp. butter. Cook about 2 minutes.

Meringue:
Beat reserved egg whites. Gradually add 12 Tbs. sugar. Pour pudding mixture into 2 deep-dish Pet-Ritz pie shells. Add meringue. Bake at 350 degrees for 15 minutes.

Margaret Leland

LEMON CHIFFON PIE

3 egg yolks, beaten
½ cup lemon juice
½ tsp. salt
1 cup sugar
1 envelope plain gelatin
¼ cup cold water
1 tsp. grated lemon rind
3 egg whites
1 (9") baked pastry shell

Combine egg yolks, lemon juice, salt, and ½ cup sugar. Cook over hot water until thick, beating with rotary beater. Soften gelatin in cold water; stir into hot egg mixture until dissolved. Add lemon rind; cool until partially set. Beat remaining sugar into stiffly beaten egg whites; fold into cooled egg mixture. Put into baked pastry shell. Chill thoroughly.

Mrs. F.H. Graham

PINEAPPLE COCONUT PIE

4 eggs
1 stick margarine
1 cup sugar
1 small can pineapple
1 can flaked coconut
2 frozen pie crusts

Beat eggs well. Melt margarine and pour into eggs. Add sugar, pineapple, and coconut and mix well. Pour into pie shells. Bake at 325 degrees for 1 hour.

Mertice Cumbee

MAMA'S CHOCOLATE PIE

1 cup sugar
3 Tbs. flour (level)
½ cup cocoa
2 eggs
1 cup whole milk
¼ stick butter, melted
1 tsp. vanilla

Mix dry ingredients; add milk, beaten eggs, and butter. Cook until thick, stirring constantly as it's easy to scorch. Add vanilla. Put in precooked pastry. Serve with Cool Whip.

Minnie Cash

PASTRY

2 cups sifted all-purpose flour
1 tsp. salt
⅔ cup shortening

Sift flour and salt together. Cut shortening with pastry blender until the mixture is the size of small peas. Sprinkle water a little at a time over the mixture while tossing quickly with a fork, until the particles stick together. Usually 4-8 tablespoons of water are required for 2 cups flour. Form pastry into a smooth ball. Wrap dough in waxed paper and chill in the refrigerator. Sprinkle flour lightly on the board and rolling pin and rub into the wood. A coarse linen kitchen towel or canvas cloth to cover the board and a "stocking" for the rolling pin will help in rolling the dough and prevent sticking without using too much flour. Roll 1" larger than pie plate. Pat out air, fold edges under and crimp. Prick crust before baking. This prevents bubbles and shrinkage.

Mertice Cumbee

Awendaw was named after a creek once used by Indians. The highway used to be a dirt road and the people used horses and wagons for transportation. The people had to go to Mt. Pleasant so they could take the ferry to Charleston. They grew a lot of their own food such as sugar cane for syrup and sugar, different fruit trees like grapes, apples, and pears. The community had a meat house to cure meat and an ice house. The ice man would go by and sell the ice for 15 cents a block. Then the people would bury it so it would stay cold underground.

Rhondell Green
McClellanville Middle School

MAMA'S FUNERAL SALAD

To everyone else, Mama called this "Bing Cherry Salad," but at home it was "Funeral Salad" because when anybody departed, it was the dish she took to the bereaved.

1 can bing cherries, drained
1 cup cubed pineapple, drained
1 pkg. red raspberry Jello
1 pkg. black cherry Jello
½ cup boiling water

Save 1 cup of the cherry juice (if not enough, add pineapple juice to make 1 cup). Dissolve Jello in boiling water; add cherry juice, cherries, and pineapple. Pour into a flat Pyrex dish or mold and chill until congealed. Serve with mayonnaise or the following dressing:
    1 pkg. cream cheese
    1 Tbs. orange juice
    ½ tsp. grated orange rind
    1 tsp. (heaping) sugar
    Pinch of salt

Whip cheese with juice and beat in other ingredients.

Adam Howard

FROZEN FRUIT SALAD

8 oz. cream cheese
¾ cup sugar
1 carton thawed frozen strawberries
1 can pineapple tidbits, undrained
2 bananas, sliced, with lemon juice sprinkled on them
½ cup chopped nuts
8 oz. carton of Cool Whip

Beat cream cheese with sugar. Add other ingredients 'til well blended. Freeze in 9" x 13" dish or pan. Cover well.

Great to keep in the freezer in hot weather!

Betty Bonner

CHERRY BERRY ON A CLOUD

The first day:
    6 egg whites
    ½ tsp. cream of tartar
    1¾ cups sugar
    ¼ tsp. salt

Beat the egg whites until foamy, add the cream of tartar and salt, and beat until you have soft peaks, almost to hard peaks. Add the sugar 2 tablespoons at a time. Beat well. Spread on a 10" circle of brown paper. Bake at 275 degrees for 1 hour. Turn off the oven. Open in the morning.

The second day:
    6 oz. cream cheese, softened
    1 tsp. vanilla
    1 cup whipping cream, whipped
    1 cup sugar
    2 cups miniature marshmallows.

Combine first 4 ingredients. Mix well. Stir in marshmallows. Spread on meringue. Refrigerate.

The third day--the day of the big feast:
  2 cups fresh strawberries
  1 (21 oz.) can cherry pie filling
  1 tsp. lemon juice
  ¼ cup sugar

Combine strawberries with sugar. Stir gently and chill. Add to cherry pie filling and lemon juice. Stir gently. Spread over cream cheese layer. Refrigerate until ready to serve.

Anne McQueen Mullikin

FRUIT DIP

½ cup sugar
2 Tbs. all-purpose flour
1 cup pineapple juice
1 egg, beaten
1 Tbs. butter or margarine
1 cup whipping cream, whipped

Combine first 5 ingredients in a heavy saucepan. Cook over medium heat, stirring constantly, until smooth and thickened. Let cool completely. Fold in whipped cream. Serve over fresh fruit.

Anne McQueen Mullikin

CRANBERRY CASSEROLE

3 cups red apples, unpeeled and chopped
2 cups raw cranberries
1 cup quick cooking oats (uncooked)
½ cup chopped nuts
⅓ cup flour
¾ cup granulated sugar
½ cup light brown sugar
1 stick melted butter or margarine

In a 2-quart casserole combine apples, cranberries, and granulated sugar. Melt butter. Add flour, brown sugar, oats, and nuts. Spread over apples and cranberries. Bake at 350 degrees from 45 minutes to 1 hour, until bubbly and light brown.

Anne McQueen Mullikin

The following recipes were prepared by Jane Wineglass at the Wedge Plantation in the 1970s on the occasion of a church festival sponsored by Richard and Tatiana Dominick, the owners of the Wedge. Various crafts were demonstrated or displayed, including quilting, basketmaking, and cooking. Games and events were organized for the children, including sack races, relays, and musical concerts. One year Jane demonstrated various ways of cooking pumpkin.

PUMPKIN CHIPS

Peel and wash 1 pumpkin. Cut into thin--very thin--strips. Soak in sugar, as much as you like, overnight. Cook on top of the stove in sugar juice, slowly, with fresh lemon and lemon juice, until tender.

Jane Wineglass

PUMPKIN PIE

2 cups canned or cooked pumpkin
1½ cups undiluted evaporated milk or heavy
   cream
¼ cup brown sugar
½ cup white sugar
½ tsp. salt
1 tsp. cinnamon
½ tsp. ginger
¼ tsp. nutmeg or allspice or both
¼ tsp. cloves
2 eggs, slightly beaten
1 (9") pie shell

Mix together all ingredients for the filling. Pour mixture into shell. Bake 15 minutes at 425 degrees. Then reduce heat to 350 degrees and bake for 45 minutes. Serve with sweetened whipped cream.

Jane Wineglass

PUMPKIN BREAD

Sift together:
    1¾ cups sifted all-purpose flour
    ¼ tsp. baking powder
    1 tsp. baking soda
    1 tsp. salt
    ½ tsp. cinnamon
    ¼ tsp. cloves

In large bowl beat until light and fluffy:
    1⅓ cup sugar
    2 eggs
    ⅓ cup soft shortening

Beat in 1 cup canned or cooked pumpkin. Mix in sifted dry ingredients in 3 additions with:
    ⅓ cup water or milk
    ½ tsp. vanilla

Fold in:
    ½ cup chopped nuts
    ⅓ cup raisins or chopped dates

Pour batter into greased 12" x 8" pan and bake 1 hour at 350 degrees.

Jane Wineglass

PUMPKIN TORTE

A midwestern state fair prize winner that is an excellent dessert for special occasions during the winter holiday season.

> Graham cracker crumbs (about 24 crackers)
> ⅓ cup sugar
> ½ cup butter (1 stick)

Mix the above ingredients and press into a 9" x 13" baking pan.

> 2 eggs, beaten
> ¾ cup sugar
> 8 oz. cream cheese, softened

Mix well and pour over graham crust. Bake 20 minutes at 350 degrees.

> 2 cups cooked pumpkin (1 lb. can)
> 3 egg yolks
> ½ cup sugar
> ½ cup milk
> ½ tsp. salt
> 1 Tbs. cinnamon

Cook, stirring, until mixture thickens. Remove from heat and add 1 envelope plain gelatin dissolved in ¼ cup cold water. Cool.

3 egg whites
¼ cup sugar

Beat and fold into pumpkin mixture. Pour over cooled baked crust. Chill. To serve, cut in squares and top each with a dollop of sweetened whipped cream.

Cindy Buscemi

They used to plant sugarcanes--not the blue one, the regular-looking one--not to do anything with, not for syrup or anything, but just to have it. We used to pull it and chew it, spit it out. When it's ripe it has a seed that's black. If the seed is green it's not ready. Those were the good old days.

Jane Wineglass

BAKED CUSTARD

1 quart milk
4 eggs, slightly beaten
¼ cup sugar
¼ tsp. salt
½ tsp. vanilla
Nutmeg

Scald milk, combine eggs, sugar, and salt; add milk slowly, stirring until sugar is dissolved, then add vanilla. Pour into custard cups and place in pan of hot water. Bake in moderate oven (350 degrees) for 25 to 30 minutes or until firm. Sprinkle with nutmeg.

Frances Scott Cain

CHARLOTTE RUSSE

½ cup cold water
1 pkg. gelatin
1 cup sweet milk
½ cup sugar
½ pint cream
2 or 3 egg whites
2 tsp. vanilla or white wine
Lady fingers

Combine ½ cup cold water and 1 pkg. gelatin. Scald 1 cup sweet milk and ½ cup sugar. Pour on gelatin and let thicken until almost firm. Whip cream and egg whites separately. Fold cream in gelatin mixture, then egg whites. When gelatin is firm, add wine or vanilla. Place lady fingers around dish. Fill with cream mixture.

Lyda Graham

MAY'S BREAD PUDDING
WITH RUM SAUCE

1 loaf bread
½ cup sugar
½ cup butter or margarine
½ cup raisins
1½ cups water
Vanilla

Soak bread in water. Add sugar, margarine, raisins, and vanilla flavoring; mix well. Pour into a 13" x 9" x 2" pan and bake at 350 degrees until brown on top. Serve with rum sauce.

Rum Sauce

¼ cup rum
1 cup sugar
3 Tbs. butter

Laura McClellan, The Crab Pot Restaurant

CHOCOLATE WAFER BANANA PUDDING

1 box Nabisco Famous Chocolate Wafers
5 long ripe bananas
Juice of 1 lemon
1 large pkg. instant vanilla pudding
1 small can crushed pineapple, drained--save juice
1 can sweetened condensed milk
2 pints whipping cream
1½ cups water (including the pineapple juice)

Slice bananas and toss with lemon juice; refrigerate. Blend pudding mix, drained pineapple, condensed milk, and juice mixture. Refrigerate until firm. Whip cream and fold into pudding mixture. Alternate layers starting with chocolate cookies and ending with crumbled cookies as a garnish.

Sherry Browne

CHOCOLATE DELIGHT

Crust:
    1 cup flour
    1 stick butter

Filling:
    8 oz. cream cheese
    1 large carton Cool Whip
    1 large pkg. chocolate instant pudding
    1 cup sugar
    1 large pkg. vanilla instant pudding
    3 cups milk

Melt butter and mix with flour to form dough to line pan. Brown at 350 degrees for 15 to 20 minutes.

Beat cream cheese and sugar until fluffy. Add ½ carton Cool Whip and spread over crust. Mix milk with chocolate and vanilla pudding. Spread on top of cream cheese mix. Spread other half of Cool Whip on top. Sprinkle with nuts if desired. Cool for 1 hour.

Rosemary Fitze

Sharing a snack at the 1991 Shrimp Festival, a
photograph by Wade Spees.

FRESH PEACH ICE CREAM

Mix together:
   1 quart mashed ripe fresh peaches
   Juice of 1½ lemons
   Pinch salt
   3 cups sugar
   1 pint whipping cream, unwhipped
   1 quart half-and-half

Refrigerate the mix for 1 day before actually making the ice cream in an ice cream freezer.

Chip Hammans

BULGARIAN APPLE NUT CAKE

3 eggs
2¼ cups sugar
1½ cups vegetable oil
1½ tsp. soda
¾ tsp. salt
3 cups all-purpose flour
3 cups chopped red apples, unpeeled
1½ cups chopped nuts

Beat together eggs, sugar, and oil. Sift flour, soda, and salt. Add to first mixture and mix well. Stir in apples and nuts. Bake in a greased bundt pan at 350 degrees for 1 hour or longer. Test. This makes a stiff batter but it's an easy recipe and very good.

Lottie Mellette, from *Minnesota Cookbook*

FRESH APPLE CAKE WITH GLAZE

1¼ cups oil
2 cups sugar
3 cups flour
1 tsp. soda
3 eggs
1 tsp. salt
1 tsp. vanilla
3 cups apples, peeled and chopped
1 cup nuts

Mix oil and sugar. Add eggs one at a time. Sift flour, soda, and salt together and add to egg mixture. Combine remaining ingredients and bake in greased tube pan. Bake at 350 degrees for 1½ hours. Cool, then glaze.

Glaze

½ cup butter
1 cup brown sugar
¼ cup Pet milk

Combine butter, brown sugar, and milk. Bring to a full boil and stir. Pour over cooled cake.

Jenna McClellan

FRESH APPLE CAKE

1½ cups Wesson oil
2 cups sugar
3 eggs
3 cups plain flour
½ tsp. salt
1 tsp. soda
2 tsp. vanilla
1 cup chopped nuts
3 cups apples, chopped

Sift flour, salt, and soda. Beat eggs well, adding sugar and oil. Add flour mixture, vanilla, nuts, and last, the apples. Bake at 350 degrees in loaf pans for 1½-2 hours. Serve with cool whip. Good plain.

Minnie Cash

FRESH PEACH CAKE

2 cups sugar
1 cup shortening or 2 sticks butter
4 eggs
4 Tbs. milk (¼ cup)
2 tsp. soda
2 cups mashed peaches (I use a blender)
1 cup pecans
2½ cups flour

Bake at 350 degrees for 25 minutes.

Frosting

1 stick butter
8 oz. cream cheese
1 box confectioners sugar
Vanilla

Chip Hammans

Helping to rebuild McClellanville after Hurricane Hugo, volunteers from a church in York, South Carolina find seats wherever they can during lunch, a photograph by Wade Spees.

MOCHA CHEESECAKE

6 oz. semisweet chocolate
1½ lb. cream cheese
½ cup sugar
⅓ cup double-strength coffee
2 large eggs
1 cup heavy cream
1 tsp. vanilla

Preheat oven to 350 degrees. Melt chocolate in double boiler. Beat together cream cheese and sugar until light. Add the eggs, one at a time, beating thoroughly after each. Beat in cream. Pour the melted chocolate slowly into the cheese mixture and add the coffee and vanilla. Mix to blend ingredients thoroughly. Pour the mixture into prepared crust, bake 45 minutes or until edges of the cake are puffed slightly. Cool to room temperature in oven with the door cracked open. Chill.

Crust

1½ cups graham cracker crumbs
¼ cup sugar
6 Tbs. butter, melted.

Place crumbs in mixing bowl, add butter and sugar, blend well. Press into bottom and up sides of a well-greased 9" springform pan. Place in freezer until ready to fill.

Margaret Densmore

CHEESECAKE

Crust:
    1¼ cups graham cracker crumbs
    ⅓ cup butter, melted
    1 Tbs. sugar

Combine and press into springform pan.

Filling:
    2 cups cottage cheese
    16 oz. cream cheese
    16 oz. sour cream
    1½ cups sugar
    4 eggs, beaten
    ½ cup butter, melted
    3 Tbs. all-purpose flour
    3 Tbs. cornstarch
    1 Tbs. plus 1 tsp. lemon juice
    1 tsp. vanilla

Blend cottage cheese in blender until smooth. Combine cottage cheese and all remaining ingredients in large mixing bowl. Beat with electric mixer until fluffy. Pour filling into crust. Bake at 325 degrees for 1 hour 20 minutes. Turn off oven and let remain in oven for 2 hours. Chill overnight.

Carrie Jean Price

GRANDMA ELLA'S COCONUT CAKE

¼ lb. butter
½ cup shortening
4 eggs
2 cups cake flour
1½ cups sugar
½ cup milk
1 tsp. vanilla
1 can Angel Flake coconut
2 tsp. baking powder

Mix all ingredients and beat constantly for 20 minutes. Use 10" tube pan or Bundt pan. Place in cold oven and set thermostat at 350 degrees. When oven registers 350 degrees start timing and bake 1 hour.

Frosting

2 cups sour cream
1 tsp. vanilla
5 cups coconut
1 cup sifted confectioners sugar

Mix sour cream, vanilla, and coconut; blend well. Add sugar to coconut mixture and blend thoroughly.

Ellen Saum, Jeremy Creek Café

OLD-FASHIONED COCONUT CAKE

2 sticks butter
2¼ cups sugar
3 eggs
3¾ cups cake flour
3 tsp. baking powder
1 tsp. salt
1½ tsp. soda (mix in buttermilk)
2¼ cups buttermilk
1 tsp. vanilla

Cream butter until fluffy. Add sugar gradually until creamy. Add eggs, one at a time. Sift flour with baking powder and salt. Add alternately with buttermilk, beginning and ending with flour. Add vanilla. Bake at 375 degrees about 25 minutes.

Frosting

3 egg whites
2¼ cups sugar
8 Tbs. water
1½ Tbs. corn syrup
1 tsp. vanilla
2 pkg. frozen coconut

Mix all ingredients except coconut in top of double boiler. Beat with electric beater until stiff peaks form (about 7 minutes or less). Add vanilla. Sprinkle 1 package of coconut between layers and 1 on outside of cake. Makes a big cake.

Betty Bonner

RUM CAKE

1 pkg. yellow or lemon cake mix
1 small pkg. instant vanilla pudding
4-5 eggs
¼ cup cold water
½ cup Mazola oil
½ cup rum
½ to 1 cup nuts

Preheat oven to 325 degrees. Generously grease bundt cake pan. Sprinkle slivered almonds, chopped pecans, or walnuts over bottom of pan. Put ingredients in large bowl in order given; beat with a whisk beater 2-3 minutes until smooth. Pour batter over nuts. Bake 45 minutes. Cool on wire rack about 5 minutes, then invert on cake plate. Using kitchen fork with long tines, pierce outside of cake to allow rum glaze to soak in.

Glaze
While cake is baking melt 1 stick margarine. Add ¼ cup water and 1 cup sugar. Bring this to a boil, stirring constantly, then cook 2½ minutes, still stirring. Remove from heat and allow to cool. Add ½ cup rum just before glazing cake. (Adding rum to hot glaze kills the taste of the rum.) Drizzle glaze over top, sides, and center of cake.
"Missie" DuPre, submitted by Barb Dubiel

MOM'S RED VELVET CAKE

1½ cups sugar
½ cup shortening
2 eggs
¼ to ½ cup cocoa
1 to 2 tsp. red coloring
2 Tbs. coffee
1 tsp. vanilla
2 cups cake flour (or less)
½ tsp. salt
1 to 1½ tsp. soda
1 cup sour milk

Cream sugar and shortening; beat in eggs, one at a time. Mix cocoa, red coloring, coffee, and vanilla together. Blend into creamed mixture. Sift flour, add salt and soda, and sift again. Add to creamed mixture alternately with sour milk. Pour into well-greased pan; bake in a 350 degree oven until sides pull away from pan.

Mertice Cumbee

ITALIAN CREAM CAKE

Cream well:
    1 stick butter
    ½ cup Crisco
    2 cups sugar
    5 egg yolks

Sift together:
    2 cups all-purpose flour
    1 tsp. soda

Add to creamed mixture 1 cup buttermilk alternately with flour and soda. Begin and end with flour.

Add:
    1 small can coconut
    1 cup chopped nuts (pecans)

Beat egg whites slightly and fold into mixture. Pour into 4 cake pans. Bake at 325 degrees for 25-30 minutes, or until cake leaves side of pans and browns.

Frosting

8 oz. cream cheese
1 stick butter
1 box confectioners sugar

Cream well together and spread on layers and sides.

Bobbie Davis

POUND CAKE

3 cups cake flour
6 eggs
2 sticks margarine
2 sticks butter
1 tsp. vanilla flavoring
3 cups sugar
1 cup milk

Cream sugar, margarine, and butter together. Add 1 egg at the time, beating after each one. Add vanilla; then add flour 1 cup at a time alternating with milk. Put in cold oven. Bake at 275 degrees for 1 hour; then turn oven to 300 degrees for 30 minutes. Let cool in pan.

"Add 'em Up"

BERTIE ROSENTHALL'S
POUND CAKE

3 cups sugar
2 sticks butter
6 eggs
3 cups flour
¼ tsp. soda
8 oz. sour cream
1 Tbs. vanilla

Cream sugar and butter; add eggs one at a time. Sift together flour and soda, and add to butter mixture. Stir in sour cream and vanilla. Bake in lightly greased and floured tube pan at 325 degrees for 1½ to 2 hours or until cake pulls away from sides of pan.

Chip Hammans

WHIPPED CREAM POUND CAKE WITH CREAM CHEESE ICING

5 large eggs (or 6 small)
3 cups sugar
3 cups cake flour
½ pint whipping cream
2 sticks pure butter
1 Tbs. Crisco
Vanilla to taste

Cream butter and sugar real good until it looks like ice cream. Add eggs, one at a time. Beat good. Add cake flour a little at a time. Add all of whipping cream at one time. Beat real good until it looks fluffy. Put in cold oven set at 325 degrees for 1 hour and 15 to 30 minutes.

Icing

1 lb. 10x sugar
4 oz. cream cheese
1 stick butter

Cream to moisten sugar. Mix thoroughly, then ice cake.

Irene Hathaway, Hathaway's Restaurant

EASY EGGLESS COCOA CAKE

1¾ cups sifted flour
1 cup sugar
¼ cup cocoa
½ tsp. salt
1 tsp. soda
1½ tsp. vanilla
1 Tbs. vinegar
⅓ cup softened butter
1 cup cold water

Combine all the dry ingredients and sift them together into a mixing bowl. Add the remaining ingredients and beat until the batter is almost smooth. Butter a 9" square pan, line it with waxed paper, and butter the paper. Pour in the batter and bake at 350 degrees for 30 minutes. Let cool before removing waxed paper. Serve either warm or cold with sweetened whipped cream, or pour chocolate glaze over cake (see following recipe) and refrigerate until glaze hardens to the consistency of cold butter.

Dale Rosengarten, adapted from *A Salute to Chocolate* by Sylvia Balser Hirsh and Morton Gill Clark (New York: Gramercy Books, 1968)

BITTERSWEET CHOCOLATE GLAZE

2 (1 oz.) squares unsweetened chocolate
2 (1 oz.) squares semisweet chocolate, or ¼
   cup chocolate pieces
¼ cup (½ stick) butter, softened and cut up
2 tsp. honey

Combine the unsweetened and semisweet chocolate, butter, and honey in the top of a double boiler and melt over hot water. Take off the heat and beat until cold but "pourable"--until it thickens. Place the cake on a rack over piece of waxed paper and pour glaze all over. Tip the cake so the glaze runs evenly over the top and down the sides. Smooth sides, if necessary, with a metal spatula. Recipe doubles easily.

Dale Rosengarten, courtesy of Kathleen Imhoff, Montevallo, Alabama

DARK CHOCOLATE CAKE

A yummy dark chocolate cake that's quick and easy to prepare.

2 cups water
½ cup vegetable oil
1 Tbs. white vinegar
2 tsp. vanilla extract
3 cups all-purpose flour
1½ cups sugar
½ cup unsweetened cocoa
1½ tsp. baking soda
½ tsp. salt

Preheat oven to 350 degrees. Grease and flour a 13" x 9" x 2" baking pan, or coat it with non-stick cooking spray. Combine first 4 ingredients in a large bowl. In a separate bowl, combine flour and next 4 ingredients; stir well. Add flour mixture to water mixture. Beat at low speed of electric mixer until well blended. Beat an additional minute at high speed. Pour batter into prepared pan. Bake at 350 degrees for 35 minutes or until toothpick inserted in center comes out clean.

Cindy Buscemi

MOCHA FUDGE FROSTING

1 stick butter or margarine
4 Tbs. unsweetened cocoa
2 Tbs. instant coffee granules
4 Tbs. milk
1 tsp. vanilla extract
1 box (16 oz.) powdered sugar, sifted
½ cup pecan pieces (optional)

Place first 4 ingredients in saucepan and boil 1½ minutes over medium heat, stirring constantly. Cool slightly; add vanilla extract and powdered sugar. If necessary, add a tiny bit more milk to reach spreading consistency. Spread warm frosting over hot cake in pan. Chopped pecans may be sprinkled on top, if desired. For more traditional chocolate frosting, omit coffee granules. For a low-cal version, cool cake completely in pan on wire rack, then sprinkle lightly with powdered sugar instead of frosting.

Cindy Buscemi

LIGHT CHEESECAKE

Make a graham cracker crust in a 9" x 13" sheet cake pan.

Dissolve and cool:
   1 (3 oz.) pkg. lemon jello in 1 cup
      boiling water.

Put 1 (13 oz.) can evaporated milk in a pan in the freezer until crystals form around the sides. Beat milk until stiff, but not as stiff as egg whites.

Cream until fluffy and light:
   8 oz. cream cheese
   Scant ¾ cup sugar

Mix jello with fluffed cheese. Fold in whipped milk. Pour in crust and refrigerate overnight before serving.

Chip Hammans

GRANDMOTHER HAMMANS' FAMOUS SOFT GINGERBREAD

½ cup sugar
1 cup sorghum molasses
½ cup butter
1 tsp. ginger
1 tsp. cinnamon
1 tsp. cloves
2 tsp. soda dissolved in 1 cup boiling coffee
2½ cups flour
1 egg, well beaten

Mix ingredients and bake at 375 degrees in cupcake pans with paper liners. Serve warm with whipped cream or an orange or lemon sauce.

Chip Hammans

GRANDADDY'S
GLORIFIED BROWNIES

1 cup sugar
½ cup butter
2 eggs
¾ cup flour
3 Tbs. cocoa
1 cup nuts
Pinch salt
24 marshmallows, cut in halves

Cream sugar and butter, add eggs. Sift flour and cocoa together, add to egg mixture; add nuts. Bake 20 minutes in shallow (9" x 12") pan. Cover hot brownies with marshmallows, then icing. Allow to cool in the pan. The heat from the brownies will melt the marshmallows. Cut in squares when cold.

Icing

2 cups powdered sugar
¼ cup butter
3 Tbs. cocoa
4 Tbs. cream

Jo Luquire

MOCK ECLAIR

Whole graham crackers
3 cups milk
2 pkgs. French vanilla instant pudding
8 oz. Cool Whip
1 can milk chocolate icing

In 9" x 13" pan, layer graham crackers. Mix the pudding with the milk, fold in the Cool Whip, and pour over crackers. Repeat above and spread 1 can chocolate icing over all. Heat icing. (I microwave mine for several minutes and then spread.) Refrigerate and cut into squares, then serve. Serves 10-12. Decadent!

Jackie Morrison, Laurel Hill Bed and Breakfast

On the weekend my grandmother had to go in the fields and plant sugar cane and corn. When the plants were grown she would get something like a sword and cut the plants down. When she died, she gave the sword to me. I treasure it.

Victoria George
McClellanville Middle School

SUGAR COOKIES

1 cup 4x sugar
2 eggs
1 cup granulated sugar
1 tsp. vanilla
1 cup margarine
1 cup salad oil
4 cups plus 4 heaping Tbs. sifted flour
1 tsp. salt
1 tsp. soda
1 tsp. cream of tartar

Mix ingredients together. Separate into 3 bowls and use food coloring to color mixtures pink, green, and yellow. Use cookie press. Bake at 350 degrees for 10 to 12 minutes.

OATMEAL/ RAISIN/ CHOCOLATE CHIP COOKIES

2 cups flour
¾ cup sugar
¾ cup brown sugar
1 tsp. baking powder
1 tsp. vanilla
1 egg
2½ cups rolled oats
1 cup raisins
2 cups chocolate chips
1 cup butter, completely melted

Combine all ingredients. Batter will be slightly stiff. Drop on a greased cookie sheet. Bake at 375 degrees for 10-12 minutes.

Phyllis Austin

KETCHUM OATMEAL COOKIES

1 cup shortening
1 cup brown sugar
1 cup granulated sugar
2 eggs, beaten
½ cup nuts
1 tsp. vanilla
1½ cups flour
1 tsp. salt
1 tsp. soda
3 cups oatmeal

Mix ingredients together. Drop onto cookie sheet. Bake at 350 degrees until browned.

Chip Hammans

SCOTCH OATMEAL COOKIES
(SOFT TYPE)

1 cup raisins
¾ cup water
1 tsp. soda
1 cup shortening
1 cup sugar
2 eggs
2 cups oatmeal
2 cups flour
1 tsp. salt

Combine raisins and water and cook 5 minutes. Drain, reserve juice. Combine 5 tablespoons raisin juice with soda. Cream shortening with sugar. Add eggs. Stir in oatmeal, salt, and cooked raisins. Add juice and soda mixture. Stir in flour. Drop 2 inches apart on cookie sheet. Bake at 350 degrees for 10 minutes. Makes 4½ dozen.

Chip Hammans

KAHLUA
FOR COFFEE OR WHITE RUSSIANS

5th vodka
3½ cups sugar
¾ cup instant coffee
2 cups water
1 tsp. vanilla extract or 1 vanilla bean

Simmer water, sugar, and coffee for 20 minutes, stirring constantly. Cool; add vanilla and vodka.

Sherry Browne

Sherry Browne takes an order over the telephone at T.W. Graham Grocery, a photograph by Bernadette Humphrey.

INDEX

Order Form

Name_____

Address_____

City_____

State_____Zip_____

Please send me the following:

_____*The McClellanville Coast* Seafood *Cookbook*

_____*The McClellanville Coast Cookbook*

_____*The Visible Village: A McClellanville Scrapbook, 1865-1945* , by William P. Baldwin

_____*Snakes in the Outhouse, and Other Causes for Wonder,* by Jay Shuler

Each book, $14.95.

Shipping and handling: $3 for up to 4 books; $1 for each additional book.

I enclose $_____

Please make checks payable to the McClellanville Arts Council and mail to PO Box 594, McClellanville, SC 29458.

Call (803) 887-3157 for information about bulk orders.